# COPYRIGHT PAGE

# ABOUT

I0171682

The Harvest Doctor is more than just a name. Harvest represents discovery, growth, and progress, no matter the environment. I develop products such as raised beds, ebooks, and other merchandise to teach and inspire people to develop their innate ability to grow food. When people connect with me on social media and consume my products, they will be inspired to grow food for themselves and for others.

Visit www.theharvestdoctor.com

Instagram: @theharvestdoctor

# GOD LOVES TO GARDEN

God. Growth. Gardening. Goals.

"God Loves to Garden" is a Christian Gardener's Planting Planner that allows the gardener to document the growth of gardens and how God grows inside us! While moving through various seasons, it can be challenging to trace the evidence of God's presence in our lives and the environment.

This book is a seven-year, thought-provoking activity planner to trace how God grows us, your garden, and the environment.

The year 2030 will have many changes to economic, technological, and societal responses to the environment. This Christian-based planting planner has inspirational quotes about God and the garden up to 2030, which will prompt the reader to imagine, wonder, and dream of one of the mysteries of the Bible, God's intentionality of the garden, and the future He plans to grow for us. These quotes help us monitor + trace God's growing activities, allowing us to better connect with ourselves, enjoy the journey with God, and grow with God in every gardening season.

ISBN: 979-8-218-22141-6

# TABLE OF CONTENTS

# GROWTH IS MY INHERITANCE.

THE PACE, RATE, AND SPACE OF MY GROWTH DEPENDS ON MY GOD-GIVEN ASSIGNMENT.

# INTRODUCTION: GOD GROWS

Have you wondered how God plans to grow you?

While caring for gardens, I experienced a stillness and calmness beyond words. In a season of obscurity, I learned how to wander + wonder. The garden is a place of joy, healing, creativity, peace, and the freedom of alone time with God.

And the girl grew (Luke 2: 52). Although this scripture describes the growth of Jesus, I could not help but wonder how God grows myself and others.

An empty garden plot is a place of obscurity and it takes gardeners to see the future and call forth an empty space to be something that is not there. However, gardeners can develop the gift of calling things into existence while looking forward to the future. This is a gift that is cultivated by God.

These Biblical growing values got me through the place of obscurity, and these are my reasons for growing gardens and sharing growth with the world.

After speaking to expert gardeners, folks too afraid to garden, and people trying to understand the place of obscurity, I realized there is a method to "Growing Through It": to grow a garden while growing YOU in Christ, from the inside/out!

# Why 2030?

God is calling us to grow more gardens because of the climate and environmental crisis.

The year 2030 is often highlighted as a significant milestone in understanding climate change and food scarcity. This planting plan is designed to trace how God grows in us so that we can become better gardeners of ourselves and for our families and communities.

By 2030, countries are expected to have implemented their commitments to reduce greenhouse gas emissions, making it a crucial year to assess progress towards these targets. You play a major role in eliminating climate change and gardeners are on the front lines. By 2030, you'll have a solid map to grow yourself in Jesus, and your garden to inspire others to do the same.

## God Cares about the Environment and Gardeners are Charged with Caring for His Creation

# The Meaning of Growth

The Bible is a book on gardening. God is very intentional about gardens, land, water, soil, weeds, trees, rivers, seed, soil, rocks, wheat, and herbs. God is a growing God.

In gardening, the Hebrew definition of growth refers to the process of plants sprouting and developing from seed. This growth process happen in gardens and is closely tied to the health and prosperity of gardeners + their families.

After completing this planting plan, you can grow food for your family, friends, surrounding community, and trace the way in which God takes us through our own growth journeys. Therefore, this planting plan is a mapping process that charts God's growing process of you and your plants to 2030.

## I Am Ready to Plan My Growth

# EVERYTHING HAS A SEASON

I appreciate the Hebrew word for seasons is "תקופות" (tekufot), which is derived from the root word "תקופה" (tekufah), meaning a period or cycle of time.

Seasons are marked by changes in temperature, weather patterns, and the natural environment and are associated with various holidays, customs, and traditions. For instance, in Jewish culture, seasons were related to different crops and agricultural practices, and many Jewish holidays were tied to the rhythms of the farming calendar. Therefore, if you know your season and define it for yourself, you'll know what to do (in the garden and in your personal life).

Overall, the Hebrew definition of seasons reflects the cyclical nature of time and the natural world's changes throughout the year. This concept is closely tied to the Jewish tradition's agricultural roots, the importance of food production, and environmental stewardship in ancient times.

# Seasons and the Eternal Calendar

Psalm 139 is one of those scriptures that speak to the eternal calendar of God. No matter my season, I think of the "You are There" perspective, giving me a glimpse of God's eternal calendar.

Where can I go from your Spirit?
  Where can I flee from your presence?

If I go up to the heavens, you are there;
  if I make my bed in the depths, you are there.

If I rise on the wings of the dawn,
  if I settle on the far side of the sea,

even there, your hand will guide me,
  your right hand will hold me fast (Psalm 139: 7-10).

Just as the seed remembers the past, God's past is your future. God remembers your entire life while you are growing through the present. Additionally, just as the seed is living off of its past, you are living off the same Word that was/is/continues to be a promise to you and your family throughout generations.

# Seasons and the Eternal Calendar

## The WILL of God Expressed

Your good garden (life) has already happened. The answer you want is older than your questions..

# ALPHA
## (BEGINNING)

# OMEGA
## (END)

Your cycles and seasons are here.
You are growing a garden here.
Your prayers for a good garden (life) are already present in eternity. Deliverance is merely the change of soil, nutrients, and location.

# Seasons and God's Timeline

God is a God of Seasons, as noted in Ecclesiastes 3 1-8. God does not place emphasis on years and months, which means our timeline may not align with God. **What do you notice about this scripture that defines and describes seasons?**

*"For everything there is a season, and a time for every matter under heaven: 2a time to be born, and a time to die; a time to plant, and a time to pluck up what is planted; 3a time to kill, and a time to heal; a time to break down, and a time to build up; 4a time to weep, and a time to laugh; a time to mourn, and a time to dance; 5a time to throw away stones, and a time to gather stones together; a time to embrace, and a time to refrain from embracing; 6a time to seek, and a time to lose; a time to keep, and a time to throw away; 7a time to tear, and a time to sew; a time to keep silence, and a time to speak; 8a time to love, and a time to hate; a time for war, and a time for peace"* (Ecclesiastes 3:1-8).

God's word does not mention calendar years, months, and deadlines. Certain conditions and events mark seasons, which can help you determine your own season. Also, these seasons are set in the binary, which means that God's timeline is set in stone to ensure the promise of all these things coming to pass (Jeremiah 33:20), including blessings of a harvest. Knowing God's times can help you better position yourself in God, especially during challenging seasons.

11

# Your Season

Typically, we understand seasons in stages such as childhood, adolescence, young adulthood, middle age, and retirement or old age, but we also experience seasons within these stages. As the position of the Earth changes, your emotions, responses, reactions, and resilience shift because we are human + our experiences shape our identity.

The shift, or between seasons, is considered a grey area or a place of obscurity and uncertainty. A collard green demonstrates this perfecting process in a gray area. The collard appears slow to grow during the REST SEASON, but something special happens deep down within it! The frost on the collard is being converted into sugar, which makes them perfect for harvest!

Therefore, the season, the number of events, and the intensity of challenges and opportunities require gardeners to adapt, learn, and grow in new ways. Embracing gardens and various crops can provide a plan to navigate unique challenges so that individuals can achieve a sense of fulfillment and meaning in their journeys.

This Christian-based gardening planting planner merges the idea of God growing plants and us simultaneously.

# Capture the Rain

Like the rain and the snow come down from heaven (Isaiah 55:10), most precipitation in various seasons behaves like the Word of God, but we have to take hold of it, no matter the season in the garden and our lives.

The Word works like this:

Falls (from heaven)
Lands
Proceeds
Does Not Return Void
Cleans
Restores
Replenishes
Preserves
Protects
Pulls Down (strongholds)
Washes Away

The Word of God does so much good for us. Therefore, it is important to have guardianship of the promise (or your garden) despite what is falling from the heavens (the life handed to you/or rain for your garden/the Word of God concerning you).

# We Choose to Grow

Growing comes with choices.

## FATE

### Without Jesus

- Whatever life gives me, I am okay with it.
- I don't have a green thumb.
- I failed at gardening last year, so I won't start another.

## DESTINY

### With Jesus

- What I have done with the will of God (God's highest desire for you).
  - Gardening is my heritage.
  - Last year was a challenging season, but I will still plant a garden again.

As God watches over his word to perform it (Jeremiah 1:12), we must be active over the promise of our gardens.

**Root word is "NOW". It can be proven.**

# Know Your Space

Practice and prayer can help you to navigate the atmosphere, environment, climate, and temperature of your garden.

ATMOSPHERE

ENVIRONMENT

CLIMATE

TEMPERATURE

These are all important elements to consider when growing a garden and growing ourselves with the help of Christ Jesus.
The atmosphere, environment, climate, and temperature impact your garden. These are all internal as well. The more chaotic your atmosphere, environment, climate, and temperature are, it could be to hear from God.

Can you listen louder than the noise?

What are some similarities and differences between the external (your garden) and the internal (you)?

# Name Your Seasons

God is a God of Seasons, as noted in Ecclesiastes 3;1-8. God does not place emphasis on years and months, but rather the **conditions** of an environment, the **duration**, and **intensity** of the experience.  Certain conditions and events mark seasons, which can help you determine your season

**Ice Season:** Also known as the freezing season. Average temperatures are below freezing. This season includes proliferation of frost, snow, and ice.

**Rest Season:** Also known as the cool season. Average high temperatures are between 35 and 65 degrees Fahrenheit. Frost and snow is common in this season.

**Promise Season:** Also known as the warm season. Average high temperature is between 65 and 85 degrees Fahrenheit.

**Harvest Season:** Also known as the hot season. Average high temperature is 85 degrees Fahrenheit and above.

# Name Your Seasons

Name your seasons. Think about what season you are in right now or past seasons. Describe the **conditions**. What is the **duration** of the experience? How **intense** is the experience? What kinds of people are **drawn** to you? What are the characteristics of people, places, + things that are **resistant** to your growth? What is your **pain point**? Name the person(s), place (s), and things(s) that **encourages** your growth?

## Notes:

17

# Draw the Arch

FIRST FROST

LAST FROST

# Draw The Arch

Harvest

Promise          Promise

FIRST FROST          LAST FROST

Rest          Rest

Ice          Ice

J F M A M J J A S O N D

Inspired by www.Gardenary.com, an arch show how the seasons progress through the year. Label parts of the arch where you are most active in your garden or expect some growing opportunities. This allows you to plan what you'll plant and grow each season.

# Your City:

**FIRST FROST** ———————————————— **LAST FROST**

**J F M A M J J A S O N D**

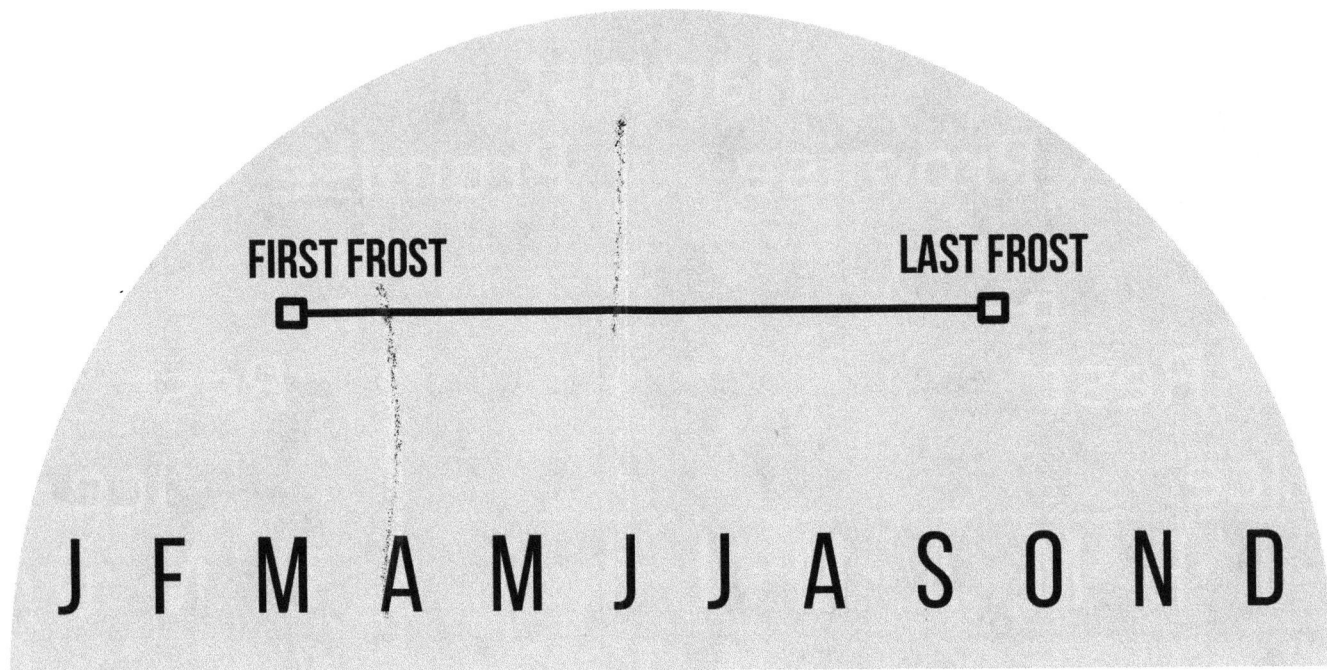

Once aligned the seasons with each month, you can plan out your garden for a year. The next step is to think carefully about what you want to grow based on the seasons.

Congratulations, you've created your own seasonal planting for you and your garden. Now, let's begin to trace God's method in growing plants and growing you.

# January

"God is sovereign over all of the elements of the Earth."

# February

"Rest in knowing seasons change. The shift means a new beginning is on the horizon."

# March

"Be like soil and intercede for yourself and others."

# April

"Growing is a life journey. The reaping of growth is a positive shift in your responses, reactions, and an increase in resilience."

# May

"Like your garden, you have a cover. You are protected."

# June

"Be more than a flower and grow beyond the outer appearance. Grow from the inside and bear fruit."

# July

"Like the aphids and deer pants for your garden, offense will come and go. Be strong and courageous. Grow Through It."

# August

"What is in you is for you, but what is on you is for others. As you harvest for yourself, give to others."

# September

"Gardening is a career of the future. You live, work, and breathe in and out of time."

# October

"Your garden is growing and you are having a grow through moment. You did it!"

# November

"Messiness works in your favor. Leave the mess and let nature care for the rest."

# December

"Your garden is in a deep state of rest in Jesus, which is a kind of growth. Grow through your seasons and rest."

*My Growing Goal:*

# How to Use This Planner

## SOW/PROPAGATE
*This section is reserved for sowing and propagating dates*

## PLANT
*Write down which seedlings were planted*

## PRUNE
*Keep track of what plants need to be cut and cultivated*

## HARVEST
*Record which plants need to be harvested*

## SCRIPTURES:
- [ ] *Write scriptures that remind you of your garden and your season*
- [ ]
- [ ]
- [ ]
- [ ]
- [ ]
- [ ]

## WEATHER NOTES
*This section is reserved for notes on temperatures and weather patterns*

## OTHER

**REMINDERS**

# Track God Growing

| DATE | CROP PLANTED IN YOUR GARDEN? | HOW DOES THE CROP REMIND YOU OF WHAT GOD IS SAYING TO YOU? | DID GOD RESOLVE THE ISSUE? |
|------|------|------|------|
| 5/30 | Collards | Stand tall like a mountain (Psalm 30) | God is still working it out |
| | | | |
| | | | |
| | | | |
| | | | |
| | | | |
| | | | |
| | | | |
| | | | |
| | | | |

# Your Grow Through

I THINK GOD IS
GROWING ME LIKE
THIS:

HE IS REALLY
GROWING ME LIKE
THIS:

# I HAVE A SEED THAT CRUSHES EVIL.

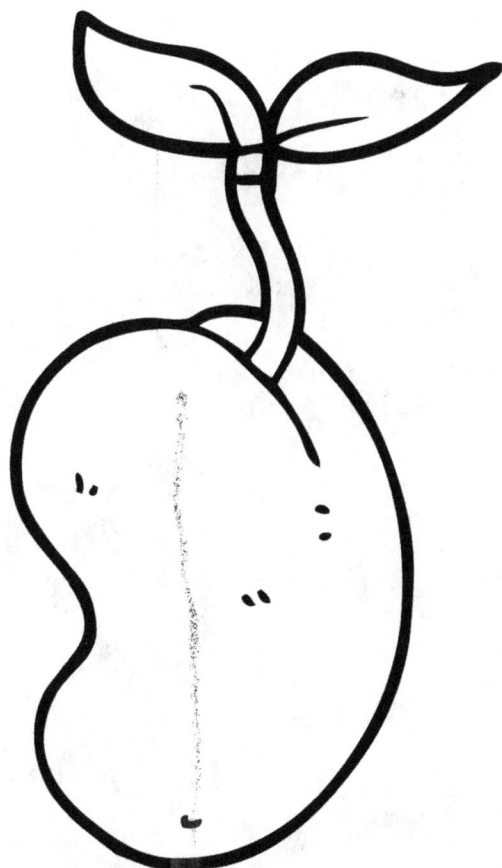

# THE ICE SEASON

By the Breath of God, Ice is Given

JOB 37:10

# PARSLEY IS A GREAT EXAMPLE OF PLANTS THRIVING IN THE ICE SEASON.

# THE ICE SEASON

The ICE SEASON is characterized as a season with average temperatures are at or below freezing. This season includes the proliferation of frost, snow, and ice.

Surviving the cold can be challenging, and keeping your mood high in a SEASON of ICE is important. Jesus specializes in mending an ICY (pride or broken) heart. This season is prone to a heart of ICE or emotional detachment or numbness, where a person may feel disconnected from their emotions or the emotions of others. God is sovereign over the all the elements, including ICE (Job 37:10). Through Jesus, He heals broken hearts through His love, compassion, and the power of His presence.

Identify the root cause of your icy heart or hard feelings. If pride and arrogance drives you, read Job 41, which lists the characteristics of a prideful, ICY heart. Identify what is causing your pride and ask God to humble you in grace and mercy. You'll tell God you cannot fix the situation by yourself and you need help. This may include reflecting on how far you've come or talking to a trusted friend, a pastor, and a therapist. The root of pride is often idolatry. Ask God to dethrone any idols and place Him at the head of every part of your life (Exodus 7:14-11:10).

God loves a broken, contrite heart (Psalm 34:18 + Psalm 51: 17). When you share with God that your heart is broken and why, your prayers are a fragrance that reaches heaven. Jesus understands the pain and sorrow associated with a broken heart. He offers comfort and compassion, providing understanding in our deepest anguish. Jesus invites us to cast our burdens upon Him and find rest for our souls (Matthew 11:28-30) so that we may grow in the future. Jesus will intercede for you + will melt your ICY heart,

Jesus is the Lamb of God with a perfect strategy for picking up the pieces of your broken heart. Through Jesus, God will remake you at the Potters house and transform you into a new person (Jeremiah18: 1-11). This includes confronting an ICY heart.

Jesus said in John 7: 38 that people who believe in Him will have rivers flowing from their bellies. There is a reason for that! Take care of your physical health by eating nutritious foods, getting enough sleep, and exercising regularly. A healthy body allows you to hear from God more clearly and eating from your garden will allow a river to flow from your belly. In addition, these activities can help improve your mood and can thaw an icy heart.

Doing activities that you enjoy and that bring you happiness can help you reconnect with positive emotions. For example, making a joyful noise and praising God is a technology that breaks the ICE SEASON (Psalm 100: 1-5).

Jesus's love is unconditional and unfailing. His love can fill the void and heal wounds caused by a broken heart or pride caused by idolatry. Through His sacrificial death on the cross, Jesus demonstrated the depth of His love for us, offering forgiveness, redemption, and a renewed sense of worth and belonging. Practicing loving others can help you reconnect with your emotions and increase your ability to connect with others. Community service at a community garden is a great way to heal a broken or prideful heart.

The ICE SEASON means the garden is gone, and gardeners can feel a sense of loss. So often, an ICY and broken hearts result from losing something (perspectives, friends, expectations, money, home, parents, trust, plants). Jesus understands the pain of loss and grief. He weeps with us in our sorrow and offers comfort in mourning. He assures us that those who mourn will be comforted (Matthew 5:4). Develop an action plan and say declarations over your ICY heart to improve your well-being. Here, you can imagine and dream of your garden.

*My ICY Heart Melts + Now I Have a River of Life Flowing From Me!*

Remember that it's okay to feel ICY sometimes, but it's important to address it if it affects your overall well-being. But God is sovereign over the ICE SEASON, as he made it with His breath. So with time, patience, and the heart of Jesus, you can find ways to reconnect with your emotions and survive the ICE SEASON.

# The ICE Season

While many vegetables can tolerate cooler temperatures, only a few can survive the ICE SEASON. These vegetables have adapted to cold climates and can remain alive and continue growing even when temperatures dip below freezing. Most of these plants are growing underground and are dormant while others grow slowly during the ICE SEASON.

## The Onion Family

Garlic, onions, chives, leeks, asparagus

These plants (some are herbs!) can be sown as bulbs or small plants in the spring or fall. They will grow and cultivate underground during the ICE SEASON. Members of this plant family such as onions and asparagus can teach us that good growth is not always seen in front of an audience. Growing while ignoring the opinions of others requires nurturing the strength to trust your own intuition, cultivate belief in God, and embrace the freedom of being rooted in your authentic self, blossoming into the best version of who you are meant to be.

No wonder the Israelites longed for members of this family such as leeks and garlic. Leeks are mentioned in the book of Numbers during the Israelites' journey in the wilderness. When the Israelites complained about their lack of variety in food, they expressed their longing for the leeks they had in Egypt, even though they were in bondage.

The significance of leeks in this context highlights the tendency to long for familiarity and comfort, even when it means being enslaved, and serves as a reminder of the Israelites' journey towards freedom and reliance on God's provision. Leeks can tolerate temperatures as low as 0°F (-18°C) and can remain in the ground throughout the winter.

Garlic is mentioned indirectly in the book of Numbers, where the Israelites express their desire for the variety of foods they had in Egypt, including garlic. The significance of garlic also symbolize the longing for the familiar and the comfort of their former life, despite being oppressed by the Egyptians. The onion family brings comfort and familiarity. Garlic can survive freezing temperatures as it is a hardy plant, but extended exposure to extreme cold can damage or kill the plant.

Asparagus should be planted in it's own raised bed and wait 2-3 years before a harvest. Like a proud asparagus, stand tall and unwavering, embracing your unique qualities, and let the world witness the strength + resilience that comes from staying true to yourself.

Just like this family, God has different growing requirements for you. Like a seed patiently unfolding, taking time to grow into your purpose in God grants you the strength to withstand storms, the wisdom to navigate challenges, and the fulfillment of blooming into the divine masterpiece you were uniquely designed to be.

## Collard Family

Brussels sprouts can tolerate temperatures as low as 20°F (-6°C) and even survive light frosts. A person in Jesus of unwavering perseverance is like the collard family, deeply rooted in resilience, standing tall amidst life's ICY conditions, and inspiring others with their unyielding spirit while maintaining a sweetness inside.

Cabbage needs a cover during the ICE SEASON and tolerates cold temperatures.

Spinach grows very slowly during the ICE SEASON. However, spinach can tolerate temperatures as low as 15°F (-9°C) and even survive heavy frosts and snow. I would use a frost cover to ensure spinach is not damaged from frost and ice. To protect and preserve other plants like broccoli and collards, wrap a string around the plant and secure it with a knot.

Not trusting God is like a plant without a frost cover. So during the ICY SEASON, find comfort + trust in Jesus.

Kale can tolerate temperatures as low as 5°F (-15°C) and can even survive heavy frosts and snow. Turnips can tolerate temperatures as low as 20°F (-6°C) and can remain in the ground through light frosts. Kale's vibrancy unbowed, whispering stories of resilience in nature's symphony of survival. Kale survives it all, just like you!

## Carrot Family

Carrots also grows very slowly during the ICE SEASON. These root vegetables can tolerate temperatures as low as 20°F (-6°C) and can remain in the ground through light frosts, but use a frost cover to ensure protection. In a harsh season's embrace, where ICY winds dance and hope recedes, carrots stand firm.

Parsnips can tolerate temperatures as low as 20°F (-6°C) and can remain in the ground through light frosts. Some members of the carrot family were mentioned in the scriptures. The Bible mentions various herbs, including parsley, mint, dill, and cumin (Matthew 23:23). Like these plants, you too can thrive in an ICY, barren place.

These hardy vegetables can be damaged or killed by prolonged exposure to freezing temperatures. Row covers or cold frames can help to extend the growing season and increase the success for growing winter vegetables in colder climates. Growing food in a raised bed is perfect because the soil in the raised bed is warmer than the Earth's soil.

# PRAYER FOR THE ICY SEASON

Dear God, you are my Alpha + Omega. You are the beginning and the end. You are the only one who can unthaw my icy heart. I cannot do this alone. So I am claiming victory over anyone or anything that is keeping my heart from you and your will for me. Although I cannot see a garden, till your purpose within me. Jesus's Name, I pray, Amen.

# YOUR PRAYER FOR

# THE SEASON

# God, Growth, + Gardens Planner

## SOW/PROPAGATE

## SCRIPTURES:

- [ ] _____
- [ ] _____
- [ ] _____
- [ ] _____
- [ ] _____
- [ ] _____
- [ ] _____

## PLANT

## PRUNE

## WEATHER NOTES

## HARVEST

## OTHER

## REMINDERS

# Track God Growing

| DATE | CROP PLANTED IN YOUR GARDEN? | HOW DOES THE CROP REMIND YOU OF WHAT GOD IS SAYING TO YOU? | DID GOD RESOLVE THE ISSUE? |
|---|---|---|---|
| | | | |
| | | | |
| | | | |
| | | | |
| | | | |
| | | | |
| | | | |
| | | | |
| | | | |
| | | | |

# Your Grow Through

**I THINK GOD IS GROWING ME LIKE THIS:**

**GOD IS REALLY GROWING ME LIKE THIS:**

# SAMPLE PLANTING PLAN

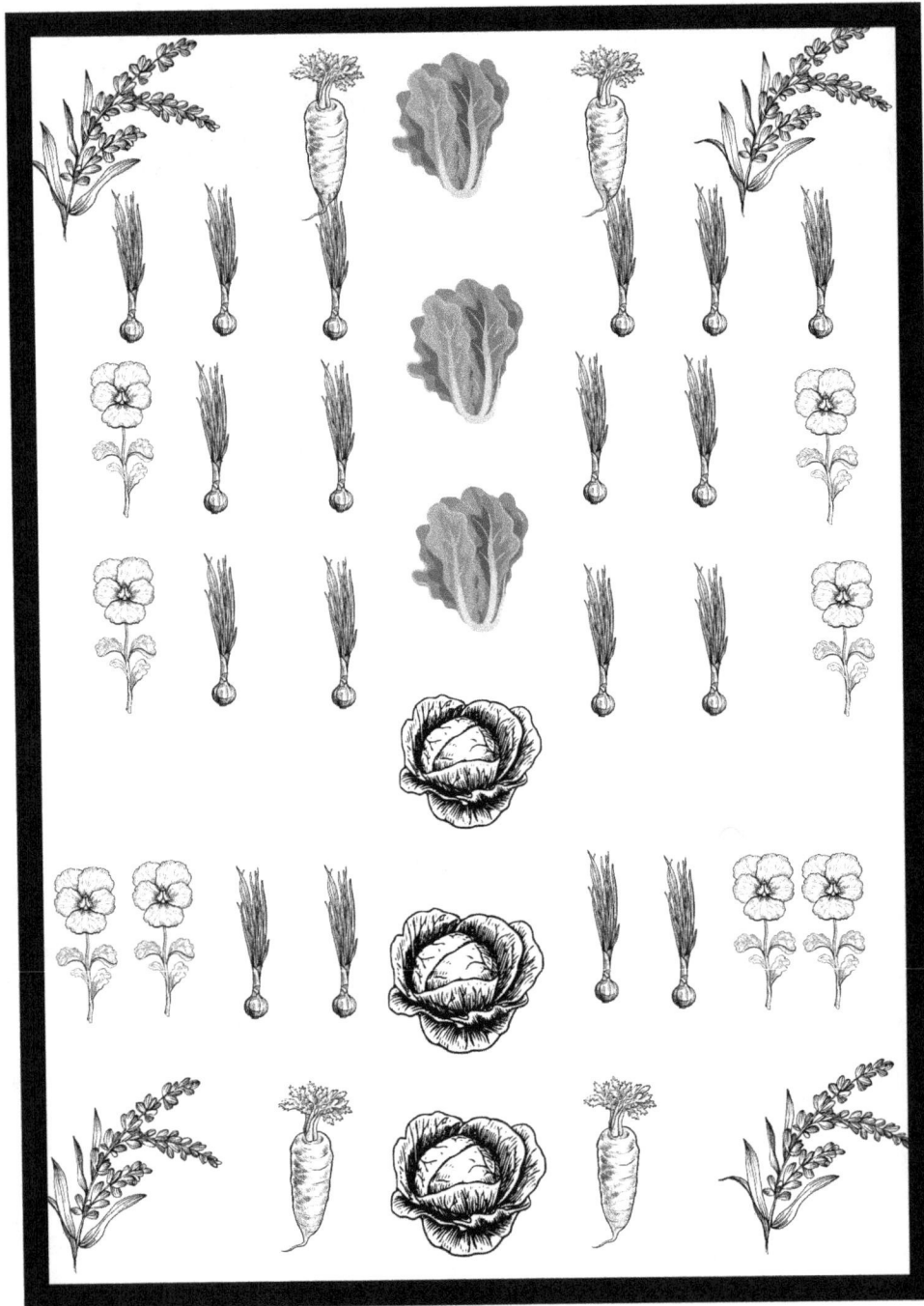

 CABBAGE

CARROTS

COLLARDS

LAVENDER

 ONIONS

 PANSY

# THE REST SEASON

Rest in the Shadow of the Almighty

**PSALM 91: 4**

# SAGE THRIVES IN THE REST SEASON AND SURVIVES THE FROST

# THE REST SEASON

The average high temperatures are between 35 and 65 degrees Fahrenheit. Frost and snow are expected in this season.

The REST SEASON means that the conditions are not suitable for gardening, but the conditions will not necessarily kill plants, although seeds may not germinate. The REST SEASON reminds me of being in a season of uncertainty or feelings of being in between seasons or stages in life. Various factors such as changes in circumstances, unexpected events, lack of direction, contradictions, or conflicting priorities can characterize the REST SEASON.

The REST SEASON also refers to calmness, peace, and relaxation. During the RESTING SEASON, I am reminded of finding rest in God, as mentioned in biblical passages like Psalm 23:2: "He makes me lie down in green pastures; he leads me beside still waters." This refers to a state of calmness, peace, and relaxation. I love this scripture for the REST SEASON because it embodies a sense of ease, spiritual connection, and detachment from the world's pressures (Satan rushes and puts pressure on you!), especially during challenging situations, knowing God is in control.

# The REST Season

While God is not the author of confusion, confusion is a sign to slow down, take a break, and hear from God. Recognize that feeling confused is a normal part of the human experience, and you should allow yourself to feel your emotions without judgment. God works with confusion to bring you deliverance + peace.

Sometimes, taking a break from your routine and getting some rest can help you clear your mind, gain perspective, and gain clarity on the next move. While taking a break, seek wisdom, encouragement, and guidance from the teachings and stories found within the Bible. Slow down any decision-making process + lean on the stories and outcomes discussed in the Bible.

Try to identify the specific area or issue that is causing your confusion or restlessness. Then, tell God why you are uncertain about the circumstances of your season. Most likely, the darkness that is before you means you are resting in the shadow of His wings (Psalm 91:4)

## I Will Rest in the Shadow of the Almighty

Set aside dedicated time each day to pray and connect with God. Share your thoughts, concerns, and be honest. God wants you to talk about the thing that deeply concerns you.

God's word in 2 Peter 3:8 says that one day to God is 1,000 years. Therefore, spending one hour with God for 24 days equals 1,000 years of walking with God.

Talking to someone you trust, such as a friend, family member, therapist, pastor, or mentor, can provide an outside perspective and help you gain clarity.

Understand that transitions, or the REST SEASON are a natural part of life, and God works in His timing. God is Lord over transitions. Trust that God has a plan for your life and that everything unfolds according to His divine will. Break down your goals into smaller, manageable steps and take action toward them. This can help you gain momentum and build confidence. Everyday is a day that you can make a small step towards clarity, understanding, and you'll be well on your way to achieving your goals. Remember Psalm 31:15 that your times (and timelines) are in the hands of God. God's goodness and mercy (Psalm 23:6) will follow you no matter the transition.

Goodness and mercy will chase you in the REST SEASON!

## Onion Family

Garlic, Chives, and onions are great for the RESTING SEASON, the season of transition. When thriving in the PROMISE + HARVEST SEASON, they repel animals from your garden.

In Numbers 11:5, the scripture says, "We remember the fish we ate in Egypt at no cost--also the cucumbers, melons, leeks, onions, and garlic". In the Old and New Testaments, this family was used as both foods and medicines that promoted digestion, healthy blood pressure, helping the immune system, and much more. The onion family are promise crops, but God promises us to grow it for ourselves and not to cultivate it while oppressed.

## Spinach Family

Swiss Chard, beets, and spinach.

Plants in this family can be planted indoors during the ICE SEASON and transported outdoors into the garden during the REST SEASON. These plants should be covered with a frost cover. This family thrives in the PROMISE SEASON. Members of this family such as spinach reminds me that HARVEST SEASON may end, but only for a little while. Swiss chard, beets, and spinach, like steadfast followers of Jesus, unfurl their vibrant foliage amidst uncertainty, teaching us to nourish our roots, adapt with grace, + to flourish during the test.

## Carrot Family

Dill, cilantro, fennel, carrots, and parsley.

The seeds of these plants can be sown during the REST SEASON, but protected under a frost cover if snow, frost, and ice are on the way. These plants can be harvested during the PROMISE and HARVEST seasons. Carrots, on the other hand, are hardy and can grow during the ICE SEASON. However, carrots need protection from frost, snow, and ice.

The Bible mentions a member of the carrot family, dill in the New Testament, specifically in Matthew 23:23, where Jesus criticizes the Pharisees and scribes for neglecting the weightier matters of the law while tithing even the smallest herbs, including dill. Jesus said, "Woe to you, scribes and Pharisees, hypocrites! For you tithe mint and dill and cumin and have neglected the weightier matters of the law: justice and mercy and faithfulness. These you ought to have done, without neglecting the others."

The identification of dill and fennel is not universally agreed upon among scholars, and there is some debate regarding its exact identity.

It's worth noting that the Bible does not extensively discuss specific herbs or spices, and these references to dill and potentially fennel (anise) are relatively brief. The primary focus of the Bible is on spiritual and moral teachings rather than botanical or culinary details. However, we cannot ignore the presence of these foods in the scriptures! Don't grow your garden just for aesthetics. The emphasis ought to be for the good of yourself, your family, and community. This connects to what Jesus meant by prioritizing moral principles and genuine righteousness over superficial displays of religious observance.

### Collard Family

Broccoli, kale, kohlrabi, cauliflower, and arugula.

Plants in this family can be planted indoors during the ICE SEASON and can be taken outdoors into the garden during the REST SEASON with a frost cover. This family also thrives in the PROMISE SEASON. Plants like broccoli take longer to grow but can hold up under frost and snow.

Let's talk about the wind's secret superpower in God's kingdom, which is common in the REST, PROMISE, + HARVEST SEASONS. When the wind caresses a delicate seedling or a fresh sprout, it's like a natural gym workout for the plant, making its stem stronger than ever. How does it happen?

The plant releases this fabulous hormone called auxin every time it dances with the wind, stimulating supportive cells' growth. Isn't that amazing? Research proves that plants exposed to the wind during their growth stage benefit from it, developing sturdier stems that won't easily topple or break. Next time you're tending to your garden, let the wind be their dance partner and witness the beauty of resilience blooming right before your eyes!

John 3:8 (NIV) Jesus spoke about the wind. He said, "The wind blows wherever it pleases. You hear its sound, but you cannot tell where it comes from or where it is going. So it is with everyone born of the Spirit" (John 3: 8). Jesus highlights the comparison between the Holy Spirit and the wind, emphasizing its invisible and unpredictable nature, its power to fill, and grow believers, and the concept of being spiritually "breathed upon" by the Holy Spirit.

Who knew that the winds grow plants like it grows us? There are also mysteries to the winds and the wave offerings. God is an amazing gardener!

**Bean and Pea Family**
Sweet peas, pole beans, Kentucky wonders, and sugar snap peas.

Plants in this family can be planted indoors during the ICE SEASON and can be transported outdoors into the garden during the REST SEASON. You can also sow seeds in the REST SEASON, but a cover may be needed if there is a danger of ice, snow, and frost. Some peas, like Sugar Snap Peas, may not thrive in the HARVEST SEASON unless planted in the shade. Other plants in this family, like Kentucky Wonders green beans, will thrive in the PROMISE SEASON and the HARVEST SEASON. The bean family may have been apart of the stew recipe that Jacob prepared for Esau in Genesis 25:30.

## Lettuce Family

The seeds of this family can be sown in the ground during the REST SEASON. I recommend keeping plants like lettuce under a frost cover. Daisies, surprisingly, are pretty hardy. A frost cover is still needed if ice and snow loom. God made all things, including delicate families like the lettuce family. They need extra protection, and it is okay to lean totally on God.

## Mint Family

Mint, thyme, sage, oregano, and rosemary.

Basil grows perfectly. This family has no problem growing towards the PROMISES of God. Most of the members of this family thrives in all four seasons. This family is also popular in the scripture. Jesus mentions how superficial displays of mint offerings cannot replace a life of righteousness.

# PRAYER FOR
# THE REST SEASON

Dear God, thank you for the love, mercy, and grace you have shown me. Thank you for the winds that heal my icy heart. I know that you are ready for me to grow into a new season, but I don't know how to grow, and I don't know what my life will look like with me as your new creature. Hold me in your hands and calm my spirit. I see you growing within me. Thank you for being my master gardener. In Jesus's name, I pray, Amen.

# YOUR PRAYER FOR
# THE SEASON

# God, Growth, + Gardens Planner

## SOW/PROPAGATE

## SCRIPTURES:

- ☐ _____
- ☐ _____
- ☐ _____
- ☐ _____
- ☐ _____
- ☐ _____
- ☐ _____

## PLANT

## PRUNE

## WEATHER NOTES

## HARVEST

## OTHER

## REMINDERS

# Track God Growing

| DATE | CROP PLANTED IN YOUR GARDEN? | HOW DOES THE CROP REMIND YOU OF WHAT GOD IS SAYING TO YOU? | DID GOD RESOLVE THE ISSUE? |
|------|------------------------------|-----------------------------------------------------------|----------------------------|
|      |                              |                                                           |                            |
|      |                              |                                                           |                            |
|      |                              |                                                           |                            |
|      |                              |                                                           |                            |
|      |                              |                                                           |                            |
|      |                              |                                                           |                            |
|      |                              |                                                           |                            |
|      |                              |                                                           |                            |
|      |                              |                                                           |                            |
|      |                              |                                                           |                            |

# Your Grow Through

I THINK GOD IS GROWING ME LIKE THIS:

GOD IS REALLY GROWING ME LIKE THIS:

# PLANTING PLANS

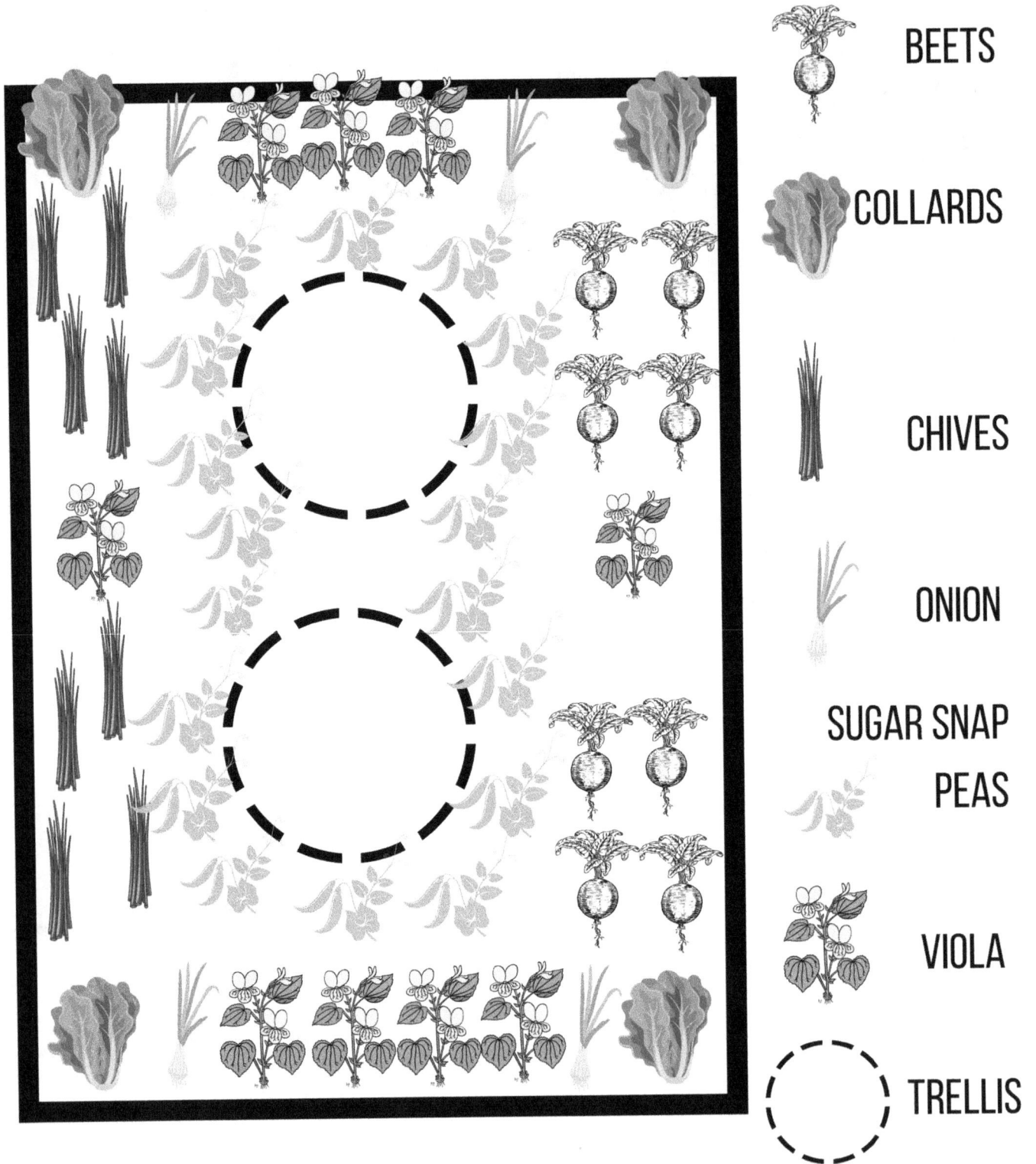

BEETS

COLLARDS

CHIVES

ONION

SUGAR SNAP
PEAS

VIOLA

TRELLIS

 COLLARDS

 KALE

LETTUCE

ONION

 PANSEY

RADISHES

# THE PROMISE SEASON

*God Promises Gardening*

**DEUTERONOMY 28: 1-14**

# ALL YOU NEED IS MUSTARD SEED FAITH FOR THE PROMISES OF GOD

# THE PROMISE SEASON

The average high temperature is between 65 and 85 degrees Fahrenheit. Frost, snow, and ice are not present in this season. Gardening is a mystery and is often used in metaphors and imagery related to gardening and agriculture to convey spiritual truths, lessons, and promises. In the Bible, God promises gardening to us, or The PROMISE SEASON forever, especially to those who love Jesus.

In Jesus's parable of the sower (Matthew 13:1-23), God is depicted as the farmer who sows seeds. Likewise, the PROMISE SEASON reminds us of the importance of receiving God's Word. As our plants grow, God's words will take root in our hearts, leading to spiritual growth and fruitfulness.

In Psalm 23:1-2, God is likened to a shepherd who provides for His people, leading them to a land full of opportunities to garden. This imagery signifies God's provision and care, just as a gardener nurtures and provides for the plants under their care. God loves the PROMISE SEASON as He loves to grow things. So as your plants grow, allow God to grow and lead you.

# The PROMISE Season

In John 15:1-2, Jesus compares Himself to the True vine of a tree, and believers are referred to as branches. Our source comes from God and ICY hearts grow when we think we are the True vine. God, the Gardener, prunes and cleanses the branches to promote growth and fruitfulness. Although cutting away people, places, and perspectives, this is God's purification, discipline, and refinement process to perfect His followers.

In Galatians 6:7-9, the apostle Paul uses agricultural imagery to illustrate the principle of reaping what we sow. He encourages believers to persist in doing good, for they will reap a harvest in due season. This teaches that our actions and choices have consequences, and God PROMISES a spiritual harvest when we faithfully sow seeds of righteousness and love. In this season, take great care of how you sow in your words and actions. Be gentle in this season of planting. You will reap what you've planted in the HARVEST SEASON.

In 2 Corinthians 5:17, believers are described as new creations in Christ, with old things passing away and everything becoming new. God will allow certain things to take place in our lives for growth into the PROMISE SEASON. Just as a seed undergoes a transformation when it sprouts and grows into a plant in the PROMISE SEASON, believers experience a spiritual transformation through faith in Christ.

## The Onion Family
Chives, garlic, and onions are your friends in this season.

They will protect your garden from enemies (bugs and animals), while spicing up your dinner!

## The Spinach Family
Swiss chard

This family can be planted in the towards the end of the REST SEASON, but they do grow faster in the PROMISE SEASON. Sow seeds indoors and transplant during the PROMISE SEASON. This family cannot thrive in the HARVEST SEASON unless planted in the shade. God created the breathtakingly vibrant Rainbow Swiss Chard, a symphony of artistic brilliance, weaving hues of beauty to inspire awe and celebrate the wonders of his creation.

## The Corn Family
Lemongrass, wheat, rice.

Sow seeds indoors and transplant into the PROMISE SEASON. They need a long time to grow, but the reward is great!

The corn family is one of the most cited in the scriptures, namely wheat! In the fields of life, Jesus tells a story about the wheat and tares, where the golden grains of righteousness stood tall, embracing the sun's grace. In contrast, the tangled tares of deceit grew along with the wheat (Matthew 13). The story of the wheat and the tares teaches us to discern the true from the false, as we nurture goodness and let love's HARVEST flourish, for in this world's ever-changing tapestry, truth and falsehood intermingle, awaiting the final separation when goodness + truth prevails.

## The Collards Family
Kale, collards, and arugula.

This family takes a short time to grow in this season. This family can be planted in the REST SEASON, but they do grow faster in the PROMISE SEASON. Many gardeners wait to harvest during the REST SEASONS so the frost can hit collards.

## The Cucumber Family
Zucchini, Squash, and Cucumbers.

This family can be planted in the towards the end of the REST SEASON, but they do grow faster in the PROMISE SEASON. If you like to sow seeds, sow indoors and transplant during the PROMISE SEASON. Set the seeds outside to get acclimated to the elements before planting. Cucumbers are also a food/fruit that the Israelites longed for during their time in the wilderness (Numbers 11:5).

## The Bean and Pea Family

Bush, Kentucky Wonders, and Pole beans

These foods will do well! These foods are promised by God!

## The Mint Family

Mint, basil, oregano, rosemary, sage, and thyme.

Plant in the PROMISE SEASON while others like mint and rosemary can be planted in the REST SEASON. Basil prefers the PROMISE and HARVEST SEASON, but does not like the ICE SEASON. It is okay to be different from your family and God made you that way! Own up to your purpose!

## Tomato Family

Peppers, eggplants, and tomatoes.

This family can be planted in the PROMISE SEASON. Sow seeds indoors and plant outside during the PROMISE SEASON. Tomatoes are often seen as my own personal PROMISE crop. While radiant from the sun, I behold the tomato's glory, a luscious orb of crimson fire, God's treasure that mirrors the resilience and richness within.

During the PROMISE SEASON, the tomato family invites us to savor life's exciting moments and embrace our own essence.

# PRAYER FOR
# THE PROMISE SEASON

Dear God, thank you for lifting me. You have grown me from an icy heart to feeling good about life, love, and adventure. Allow me to grow in humility and prepare me to receive any good thing you have for me. Lord, my garden is beautiful. Help me to have ears and a heart that hears you so that I may care for the garden you've given me to borrow. In Jesus's name, I pray, Amen.

# YOUR PRAYER FOR

# THE SEASON

# God, Growth, + Gardens Planner

## SOW/PROPAGATE

## SCRIPTURES:

- [ ] _____
- [ ] _____
- [ ] _____
- [ ] _____
- [ ] _____
- [ ] _____
- [ ] _____

## PLANT

## PRUNE

## WEATHER NOTES

## HARVEST

## OTHER

## REMINDERS

# Track God Growing

| DATE | CROP PLANTED IN YOUR GARDEN? | HOW DOES THE CROP REMIND YOU OF WHAT GOD IS SAYING TO YOU? | DID GOD RESOLVE THE ISSUE? |
|---|---|---|---|
| | | | |
| | | | |
| | | | |
| | | | |
| | | | |
| | | | |
| | | | |
| | | | |
| | | | |
| | | | |

# Your Grow Through

| I THINK GOD IS GROWING ME LIKE THIS: | GOD IS REALLY GROWING ME LIKE THIS: |
| --- | --- |
|  |  |

# PLANTING PLANS

CHERRY
TOMATOES

COLLARDS

PETUNIAS

SQUASH

ZINNIAS

TRELLIS

KALE

ONIONS

TOMATOES

MARIGOLDS

ZINNIAS

TRELLIS

 BASIL

 COLLARDS

 LETTUCE

 OREGANO

 PETUNIAS

 THYME

IS GREAT, TOO!

# THE HARVEST

# SEASON

## Fields of Golden Grain

May there be an abundance of grain swaying in the breeze, and may you blossom in the cities like the grass of the field.

## PSALM 72: 16

# THE HARVEST IS EVIDENCE OF GOD'S GROWTH PRINCIPLES IN ACTION

A growing Christian gardener maybe growing, but he/she/they remain humble and are tender/gentle in spirit (Philippians 4:5).

While the culture says to "play it big", the scripture says "don't despise small beginnings" (Zachariah 4:10). The harvest begins small, but in due season, it can feed families.

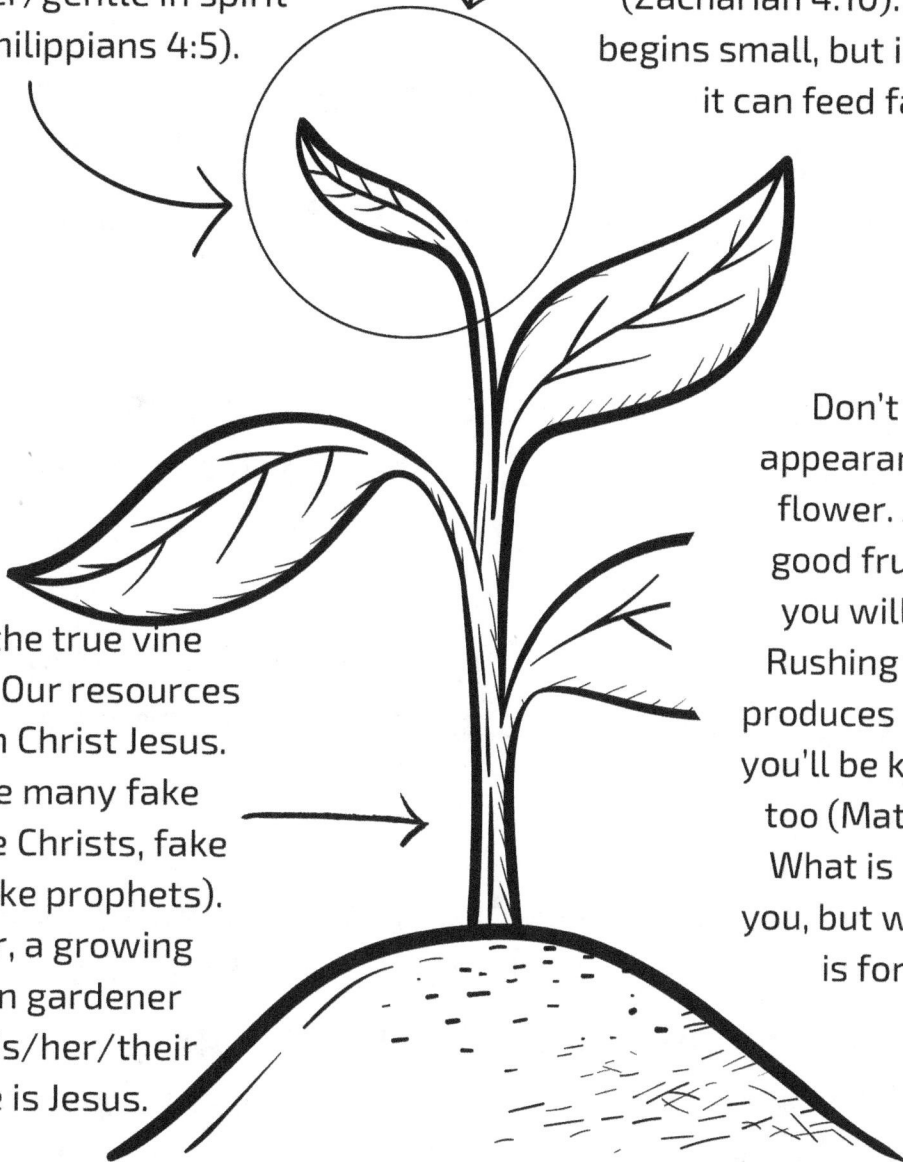

Don't strive for appearances, like the flower. Aim to bear good fruit for which you will be known. Rushing the process produces bad fruit, and you'll be known by that too (Matthew 7:16). What is in you is for you, but what is on you is for others.

Jesus is the true vine (John 15:1). Our resources come from Christ Jesus. There are many fake vines (fake Christs, fake friends, fake prophets). However, a growing Christian gardener knows his/her/their source is Jesus.

Growth begins in darkness and the seed carries revelation, which will defeat evil (Genesis 3:15). The promise is given before the foundations of the Earth The goal is to take root, stretch out, stand strong on your foundations, and expand before growing up and out. Can you grow without an audience or the approval of others?

# THE HARVEST SEASON

The average high temperature is 85 degrees Fahrenheit and above. Frost, snow, and ice does not occur in this season. This SEASON of HARVEST and the threshing floor has spiritual significance.

In Matthew 13:39, Jesus speaks of the harvest as the end of the age when the angels will separate the good and the bad. As you harvest food from your garden, you will separate the leaves, fruit, and roots you consume, and the bad harvest will be thrown into the compost. This signifies the culmination of God's plan for your life and the process in which he will prepare you.

In Joel 2:24, God promises His people an abundant harvest, symbolizing His blessings and provision, which is a place for you to grow and thrive. God promises more gardens and more territories for you to increase and live out your purpose. The reward of reaping good seeds will be God's restoration, peace beyond understanding (Philippians 4:7), and blessings upon His faithful gardeners and followers.

*Jesus has Prepared a Place For You*

# The HARVEST Season

In Proverbs 3:9-10, believers are encouraged to honor God with their wealth and the first fruits of their produce. This includes bringing offerings and tithes to the "threshing floor," which was a place where grain was separated from the chaff. Harvest-ready leaves, fruit, and roots are the first fruits in your garden for the HARVEST SEASON and should be dedicated back to God. It symbolizes dedicating the best of what one has to God.

The threshing floor is often associated with testing, refining, and purification. In Isaiah 41:15-16, God promises to make His people into a new, sharp, and threshing instrument, to thresh mountains and make them like chaff. We love the harvest, but many Christians avoid the threshing floor. A threshing floor is a place where you are separated from people, places, perspectives, and things that no longer serve you. It calls you out of the group to transform you into your new nature in Christ Jesus.

## The Harvest Season will Call You Out to Bring You In

The harvest and the threshing floor are also associated with gathering and celebration. In Jeremiah 51:33, God declares that harvest has come, and the people will rejoice. In the HARVEST SEASON, your home will be filled with joy because of the new foods and ecosystem you created for yourself and your family. You will share the joy of growing food with your neighbors and community members.

Others will catch onto the joy of gardening, God's PROMISES, and its benefits. Therefore, more gardens will emerge because you decided to walk into the growth promises. This speaks of the joy and celebration when God's promises are fulfilled.

# THE HARVEST SEASON

## The Spinach Family
Swiss chard

This family can be planted in the towards the end of the REST SEASON, but they do grow faster in the PROMISE SEASON. Sow seeds indoors and transplant during the PROMISE SEASON. Do not plant this family during the high heat of the season because it will go to seed. Swiss Chard will thrive in the shade or part shade. God's love for colorful swiss chard is like a vibrant kaleidoscope of nourishment and beauty, embracing diversity and delighting in the flavors of life.

## The Corn Family
Corn does well in the HARVEST SEASON. It grows up to the sky, looking towards the hills whence comes our help (Psalm 121: 1-2). The wheat embodies the HARVEST, but it must be placed on the threshing floor.

## The Collards Family
Kale, collards and arugula.

This family can be planted in the REST SEASON, but they do grow faster in the PROMISE SEASON. Spinach will go to seed in the HARVEST SEASON, but the collard family will keep thriving. The collard family stays planted like a tree by streams of water (Psalm 1: 3).

### The Cucumber Family
Zucchini, Squash, and Cucumbers.

This family can be planted in the towards the end of the REST SEASON, but they do grow faster in the HARVEST SEASON. Sow seeds indoors and transplant during the PROMISE SEASON. Be sure to cut the flowers for two weeks after planting so the plants can establish a strong root system. This reminds me about the ways in which God cuts things out of our lives for the purpose of growing!

### The Bean and Pea Family
Bush, Kentucky Wonders, and Pole beans

This family love the HARVEST SEASON but with regular water. Members of this family such as Kentucky Wonders are a blessing to your garden during the HARVEST SEASON. Just as green beans enrich the soil with nitrogen, God's nourishment fills our hearts and souls, rejuvenating us with love and sustenance for growth.

### The Mint Family
Mint, basil, oregano, rosemary, sage, and thyme.

Plant in the PROMISE SEASON while others like mint and rosemary can be planted in the REST SEASON. Basil prefers the PROMISE and HARVEST SEASON. Mint spreads and will take over other plants.

## Tomato Family
Peppers, eggplants, and tomatoes

This family is perfect in the HARVEST SEASON. Like the cucumber family, be sure to clip the flowers for two weeks after planting. This allows for a strong root system to establish.

## Cotton Family
Okra, cotton, and hibiscus

Start indoors in the PROMISE SEASON and transplanted to the HARVEST SEASON.

## Potato Family
Sweet Potato love the HARVEST SEASON, but needs regular watering.

# PRAYER FOR THE HARVEST SEASON

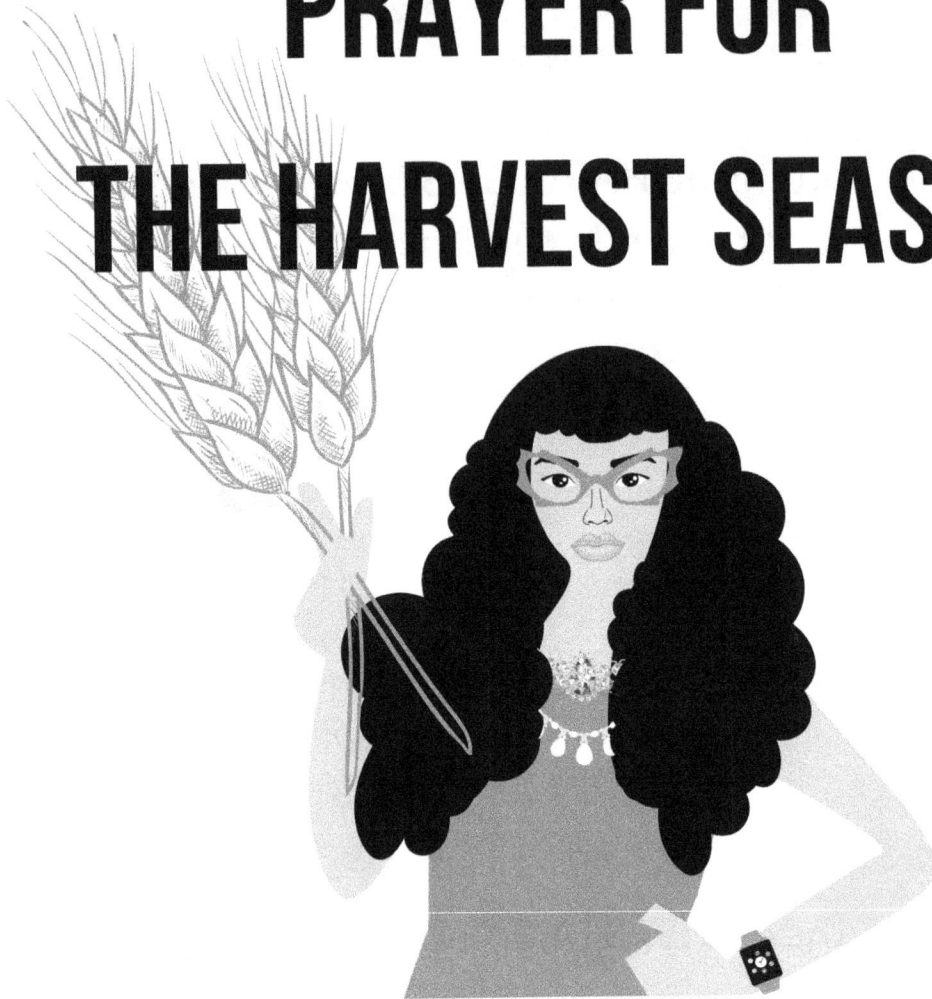

Dear God, I am ready to walk into the purpose you have for me. During harvest + sifting, hold me in your right hand. While I am thankful + joyful for my harvest, it will not come in between our connection because you are my one true God. Lord, prune my garden and separate me from anyone or anything that harms my future in Christ Jesus. Thank you for the harvest. In Jesus's name, Amen.

# YOUR PRAYER FOR

# THE SEASON

# God, Growth, + Gardens Planner

## SOW/PROPAGATE

## SCRIPTURES:

- [ ] _____
- [ ] _____
- [ ] _____
- [ ] _____
- [ ] _____
- [ ] _____
- [ ] _____

PLANT

PRUNE

### WEATHER NOTES

HARVEST

OTHER

### REMINDERS

# Track God Growing

| DATE | CROP PLANTED IN YOUR GARDEN? | HOW DOES THE CROP REMIND YOU OF WHAT GOD IS SAYING TO YOU? | DID GOD RESOLVE THE ISSUE? |
|------|------|------|------|
|      |      |      |      |
|      |      |      |      |
|      |      |      |      |
|      |      |      |      |
|      |      |      |      |
|      |      |      |      |
|      |      |      |      |
|      |      |      |      |
|      |      |      |      |
|      |      |      |      |

# Your Grow Through

I THINK GOD IS
GROWING ME LIKE
THIS:

HE IS REALLY
GROWING ME LIKE
THIS:

# PLANTING PLAN

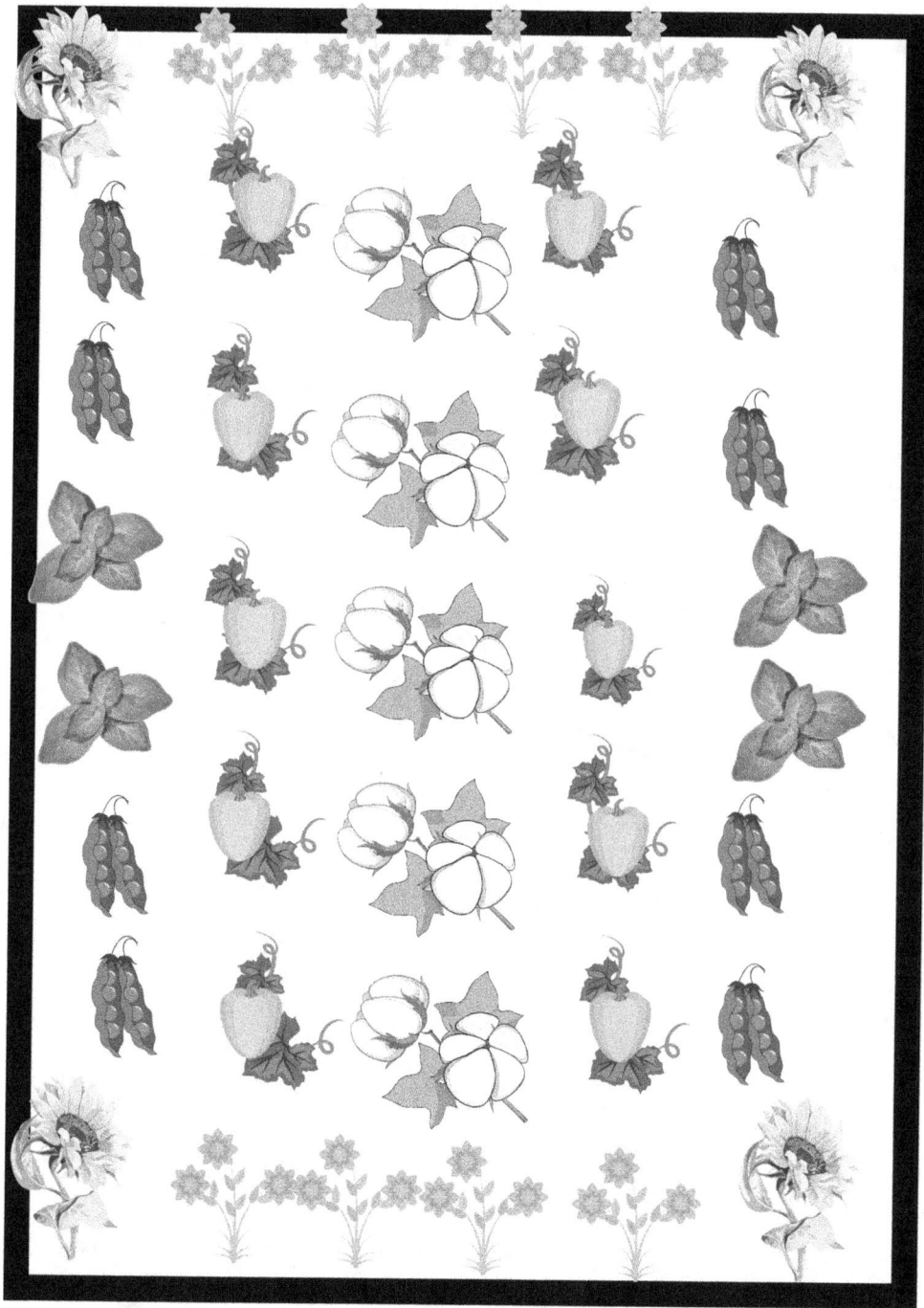

 BASIL

 LIMA BEANS

COTTON

 PEPPERS

 PETUNIAS

SUNFLOWERS

FRUIT IS STILL FRUIT, EVEN IF IT IS UNRIPEN. IT HAS TO GROW TO GET BETTER.

IT IS A GROWING PROCESS.

# Grow Calendar

## 2023-2030

# Your Blessing is Growing *Through* You

## July

| S | M | T | W | T | F | S |
|---|---|---|---|---|---|---|
|   |   |   |   |   |   | 1 |
| 2 | 3 | 4 | 5 | 6 | 7 | 8 |
| 9 | 10 | 11 | 12 | 13 | 14 | 15 |
| 16 | 17 | 18 | 19 | 20 | 21 | 22 |
| 23 | 24 | 25 | 26 | 27 | 28 | 29 |
| 30 | 31 |   |   |   |   |   |

## August

| S | M | T | W | T | F | S |
|---|---|---|---|---|---|---|
|   |   | 1 | 2 | 3 | 4 | 5 |
| 6 | 7 | 8 | 9 | 10 | 11 | 12 |
| 13 | 14 | 15 | 16 | 17 | 18 | 19 |
| 20 | 21 | 22 | 23 | 24 | 25 | 26 |
| 27 | 28 | 29 | 30 | 31 |   |   |

## September

| S | M | T | W | T | F | S |
|---|---|---|---|---|---|---|
|   |   |   |   |   | 1 | 2 |
| 3 | 4 | 5 | 6 | 7 | 8 | 9 |
| 10 | 11 | 12 | 13 | 14 | 15 | 16 |
| 17 | 18 | 19 | 20 | 21 | 22 | 23 |
| 24 | 25 | 26 | 27 | 28 | 29 | 30 |

# Your Blessing is *Around* You

## October

| S | M | T | W | T | F | S |
|---|---|---|---|---|---|---|
| 1 | 2 | 3 | 4 | 5 | 6 | 7 |
| 8 | 9 | 10 | 11 | 12 | 13 | 14 |
| 15 | 16 | 17 | 18 | 19 | 20 | 21 |
| 22 | 23 | 24 | 25 | 26 | 27 | 28 |
| 29 | 30 | 31 |   |   |   |   |

## November

| S | M | T | W | T | F | S |
|---|---|---|---|---|---|---|
|   |   |   | 1 | 2 | 3 | 4 |
| 5 | 6 | 7 | 8 | 9 | 10 | 11 |
| 12 | 13 | 14 | 15 | 16 | 17 | 18 |
| 19 | 20 | 21 | 22 | 23 | 24 | 25 |
| 26 | 27 | 28 | 29 | 30 |   |   |

## December

| S | M | T | W | T | F | S |
|---|---|---|---|---|---|---|
|   |   |   |   |   | 1 | 2 |
| 3 | 4 | 5 | 6 | 7 | 8 | 9 |
| 10 | 11 | 12 | 13 | 14 | 15 | 16 |
| 17 | 18 | 19 | 20 | 21 | 22 | 23 |
| 24 | 25 | 26 | 27 | 28 | 29 | 30 |
| 31 |   |   |   |   |   |   |

# 2023

# God's Dream For Me + My Garden

_____

_____

_____

_____

_____

_____

_____

_____

_____

_____

_____

_____

_____

# God's Promise for Me is *Gardening*

## January

| S | M | T | W | T | F | S |
|---|---|---|---|---|---|---|
|   | 1 | 2 | 3 | 4 | 5 | 6 |
| 7 | 8 | 9 | 10 | 11 | 12 | 13 |
| 14 | 15 | 16 | 17 | 18 | 19 | 20 |
| 21 | 22 | 23 | 24 | 25 | 26 | 27 |
| 28 | 29 | 30 | 31 |   |   |   |

## February

| S | M | T | W | T | F | S |
|---|---|---|---|---|---|---|
|   |   |   |   | 1 | 2 | 3 |
| 4 | 5 | 6 | 7 | 8 | 9 | 10 |
| 11 | 12 | 13 | 14 | 15 | 16 | 17 |
| 18 | 19 | 20 | 21 | 22 | 23 | 24 |
| 25 | 26 | 27 | 28 | 29 |   |   |

## March

| S | M | T | W | T | F | S |
|---|---|---|---|---|---|---|
|   |   |   |   |   | 1 | 2 |
| 3 | 4 | 5 | 6 | 7 | 8 | 9 |
| 10 | 11 | 12 | 13 | 14 | 15 | 16 |
| 17 | 18 | 19 | 20 | 21 | 22 | 23 |
| 24 | 25 | 26 | 27 | 28 | 29 | 30 |
| 31 |   |   |   |   |   |   |

# I Serve a God that *Grows*

## April

| S | M | T | W | T | F | S |
|---|---|---|---|---|---|---|
|   | 1 | 2 | 3 | 4 | 5 | 6 |
| 7 | 8 | 9 | 10 | 11 | 12 | 13 |
| 14 | 15 | 16 | 17 | 18 | 19 | 20 |
| 21 | 22 | 23 | 24 | 25 | 26 | 27 |
| 28 | 29 | 30 |   |   |   |   |

## May

| S | M | T | W | T | F | S |
|---|---|---|---|---|---|---|
|   |   |   | 1 | 2 | 3 | 4 |
| 5 | 6 | 7 | 8 | 9 | 10 | 11 |
| 12 | 13 | 14 | 15 | 16 | 17 | 18 |
| 19 | 20 | 21 | 22 | 23 | 24 | 25 |
| 26 | 27 | 28 | 29 | 30 | 31 |   |

## June

| S | M | T | W | T | F | S |
|---|---|---|---|---|---|---|
|   |   |   |   |   |   | 1 |
| 2 | 3 | 4 | 5 | 6 | 7 | 8 |
| 9 | 10 | 11 | 12 | 13 | 14 | 15 |
| 16 | 17 | 18 | 19 | 20 | 21 | 22 |
| 23 | 24 | 25 | 26 | 27 | 28 | 29 |
| 30 |   |   |   |   |   |   |

# 2024

# If I am going to *Grow*, I Need God

## July

| S | M | T | W | T | F | S |
|---|---|---|---|---|---|---|
|   | 1 | 2 | 3 | 4 | 5 | 6 |
| 7 | 8 | 9 | 10 | 11 | 12 | 13 |
| 14 | 15 | 16 | 17 | 18 | 19 | 20 |
| 21 | 22 | 23 | 24 | 25 | 26 | 27 |
| 28 | 29 | 30 | 31 |   |   |   |

## August

| S | M | T | W | T | F | S |
|---|---|---|---|---|---|---|
|   |   |   |   | 1 | 2 | 3 |
| 4 | 5 | 6 | 7 | 8 | 9 | 10 |
| 11 | 12 | 13 | 14 | 15 | 16 | 17 |
| 18 | 19 | 20 | 21 | 22 | 23 | 24 |
| 25 | 26 | 27 | 28 | 29 | 30 | 31 |

## September

| S | M | T | W | T | F | S |
|---|---|---|---|---|---|---|
| 1 | 2 | 3 | 4 | 5 | 6 | 7 |
| 8 | 9 | 10 | 11 | 12 | 13 | 14 |
| 15 | 16 | 17 | 18 | 19 | 20 | 21 |
| 22 | 23 | 24 | 25 | 26 | 27 | 28 |
| 29 | 30 |   |   |   |   |   |

## God is the *Gardener* That Tills in Me

## October

| S | M | T | W | T | F | S |
|---|---|---|---|---|---|---|
|   |   | 1 | 2 | 3 | 4 | 5 |
| 6 | 7 | 8 | 9 | 10 | 11 | 12 |
| 13 | 14 | 15 | 16 | 17 | 18 | 19 |
| 20 | 21 | 22 | 23 | 24 | 25 | 26 |
| 27 | 28 | 29 | 30 | 31 |   |   |

## November

| S | M | T | W | T | F | S |
|---|---|---|---|---|---|---|
|   |   |   |   |   | 1 | 2 |
| 3 | 4 | 5 | 6 | 7 | 8 | 9 |
| 10 | 11 | 12 | 13 | 14 | 15 | 16 |
| 17 | 18 | 19 | 20 | 21 | 22 | 23 |
| 24 | 25 | 26 | 27 | 28 | 29 | 30 |

## December

| S | M | T | W | T | F | S |
|---|---|---|---|---|---|---|
| 1 | 2 | 3 | 4 | 5 | 6 | 7 |
| 8 | 9 | 10 | 11 | 12 | 13 | 14 |
| 15 | 16 | 17 | 18 | 19 | 20 | 21 |
| 22 | 23 | 24 | 25 | 26 | 27 | 28 |
| 29 | 30 | 31 |   |   |   |   |

# 2024

# God's Dream for Me + My Garden

_____

_____

_____

_____

_____

_____

_____

_____

_____

_____

_____

_____

_____

# Jesus is My *Master* Gardener

## January

| S | M | T | W | T | F | S |
|---|---|---|---|---|---|---|
|   |   |   | 1 | 2 | 3 | 4 |
| 5 | 6 | 7 | 8 | 9 | 10 | 11 |
| 12 | 13 | 14 | 15 | 16 | 17 | 18 |
| 19 | 20 | 21 | 22 | 23 | 24 | 25 |
| 26 | 27 | 28 | 29 | 30 | 31 |   |

## February

| S | M | T | W | T | F | S |
|---|---|---|---|---|---|---|
|   |   |   |   |   |   | 1 |
| 2 | 3 | 4 | 5 | 6 | 7 | 8 |
| 9 | 10 | 11 | 12 | 13 | 14 | 15 |
| 16 | 17 | 18 | 19 | 20 | 21 | 22 |
| 23 | 24 | 25 | 26 | 27 | 28 |   |

## March

| S | M | T | W | T | F | S |
|---|---|---|---|---|---|---|
|   |   |   |   |   |   | 1 |
| 2 | 3 | 4 | 5 | 6 | 7 | 8 |
| 9 | 10 | 11 | 12 | 13 | 14 | 15 |
| 16 | 17 | 18 | 19 | 20 | 21 | 22 |
| 23 | 24 | 25 | 26 | 27 | 28 | 29 |
| 30 | 31 |   |   |   |   |   |

# My Harvest Will Beautifully *Overtake* Me

## April

| S | M | T | W | T | F | S |
|---|---|---|---|---|---|---|
|   |   | 1 | 2 | 3 | 4 | 5 |
| 6 | 7 | 8 | 9 | 10 | 11 | 12 |
| 13 | 14 | 15 | 16 | 17 | 18 | 19 |
| 20 | 21 | 22 | 23 | 24 | 25 | 26 |
| 27 | 28 | 29 | 30 |   |   |   |

## May

| S | M | T | W | T | F | S |
|---|---|---|---|---|---|---|
|   |   |   |   | 1 | 2 | 3 |
| 4 | 5 | 6 | 7 | 8 | 9 | 10 |
| 11 | 12 | 13 | 14 | 15 | 16 | 17 |
| 18 | 19 | 20 | 21 | 22 | 23 | 24 |
| 25 | 26 | 27 | 28 | 29 | 30 | 31 |

## June

| S | M | T | W | T | F | S |
|---|---|---|---|---|---|---|
| 1 | 2 | 3 | 4 | 5 | 6 | 7 |
| 8 | 9 | 10 | 11 | 12 | 13 | 14 |
| 15 | 16 | 17 | 18 | 19 | 20 | 21 |
| 22 | 23 | 24 | 25 | 26 | 27 | 28 |
| 29 | 30 |   |   |   |   |   |

# 2025

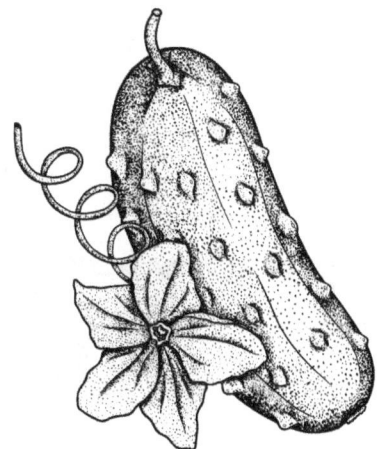

# God *Loves* To Grow Me

## July

| S | M | T | W | T | F | S |
|---|---|---|---|---|---|---|
|  |  | 1 | 2 | 3 | 4 | 5 |
| 6 | 7 | 8 | 9 | 10 | 11 | 12 |
| 13 | 14 | 15 | 16 | 17 | 18 | 19 |
| 20 | 21 | 22 | 23 | 24 | 25 | 26 |
| 27 | 28 | 29 | 30 | 31 |  |  |

## August

| S | M | T | W | T | F | S |
|---|---|---|---|---|---|---|
|  |  |  |  |  | 1 | 2 |
| 3 | 4 | 5 | 6 | 7 | 8 | 9 |
| 10 | 11 | 12 | 13 | 14 | 15 | 16 |
| 17 | 18 | 19 | 20 | 21 | 22 | 23 |
| 24 | 25 | 26 | 27 | 28 | 29 | 30 |
| 31 |  |  |  |  |  |  |

## September

| S | M | T | W | T | F | S |
|---|---|---|---|---|---|---|
|  | 1 | 2 | 3 | 4 | 5 | 6 |
| 7 | 8 | 9 | 10 | 11 | 12 | 13 |
| 14 | 15 | 16 | 17 | 18 | 19 | 20 |
| 21 | 22 | 23 | 24 | 25 | 26 | 27 |
| 28 | 29 | 30 |  |  |  |  |

## Wherever I am, I have to *Grow* More

## October

| S | M | T | W | T | F | S |
|---|---|---|---|---|---|---|
|  |  |  | 1 | 2 | 3 | 4 |
| 5 | 6 | 7 | 8 | 9 | 10 | 11 |
| 12 | 13 | 14 | 15 | 16 | 17 | 18 |
| 19 | 20 | 21 | 22 | 23 | 24 | 25 |
| 26 | 27 | 28 | 29 | 30 | 31 |  |

## November

| S | M | T | W | T | F | S |
|---|---|---|---|---|---|---|
|  |  |  |  |  |  | 1 |
| 2 | 3 | 4 | 5 | 6 | 7 | 8 |
| 9 | 10 | 11 | 12 | 13 | 14 | 15 |
| 16 | 17 | 18 | 19 | 20 | 21 | 22 |
| 23 | 24 | 25 | 26 | 27 | 28 | 29 |
| 30 |  |  |  |  |  |  |

## December

| S | M | T | W | T | F | S |
|---|---|---|---|---|---|---|
|  | 1 | 2 | 3 | 4 | 5 | 6 |
| 7 | 8 | 9 | 10 | 11 | 12 | 13 |
| 14 | 15 | 16 | 17 | 18 | 19 | 20 |
| 21 | 22 | 23 | 24 | 25 | 26 | 27 |
| 28 | 29 | 30 | 31 |  |  |  |

# 2025

# God's Dream For Me + My Garden

# Repentance is *Pruning*

## January

| S | M | T | W | T | F | S |
|---|---|---|---|---|---|---|
|   |   |   |   | 1 | 2 | 3 |
| 4 | 5 | 6 | 7 | 8 | 9 | 10 |
| 11 | 12 | 13 | 14 | 15 | 16 | 17 |
| 18 | 19 | 20 | 21 | 22 | 23 | 24 |
| 25 | 26 | 27 | 28 | 29 | 30 | 31 |

## February

| S | M | T | W | T | F | S |
|---|---|---|---|---|---|---|
| 1 | 2 | 3 | 4 | 5 | 6 | 7 |
| 8 | 9 | 10 | 11 | 12 | 13 | 14 |
| 15 | 16 | 17 | 18 | 19 | 20 | 21 |
| 22 | 23 | 24 | 25 | 26 | 27 | 28 |

## March

| S | M | T | W | T | F | S |
|---|---|---|---|---|---|---|
| 1 | 2 | 3 | 4 | 5 | 6 | 7 |
| 8 | 9 | 10 | 11 | 12 | 13 | 14 |
| 15 | 16 | 17 | 18 | 19 | 20 | 21 |
| 22 | 23 | 24 | 25 | 26 | 27 | 28 |
| 29 | 30 | 31 |   |   |   |   |

# Growth is My Warfare *Weapon*

## April

| S | M | T | W | T | F | S |
|---|---|---|---|---|---|---|
|   |   |   | 1 | 2 | 3 | 4 |
| 5 | 6 | 7 | 8 | 9 | 10 | 11 |
| 12 | 13 | 14 | 15 | 16 | 17 | 18 |
| 19 | 20 | 21 | 22 | 23 | 24 | 25 |
| 26 | 27 | 28 | 29 | 30 |   |   |

## May

| S | M | T | W | T | F | S |
|---|---|---|---|---|---|---|
|   |   |   |   |   | 1 | 2 |
| 3 | 4 | 5 | 6 | 7 | 8 | 9 |
| 10 | 11 | 12 | 13 | 14 | 15 | 16 |
| 17 | 18 | 19 | 20 | 21 | 22 | 23 |
| 24 | 25 | 26 | 27 | 28 | 29 | 30 |
| 31 |   |   |   |   |   |   |

## June

| S | M | T | W | T | F | S |
|---|---|---|---|---|---|---|
|   | 1 | 2 | 3 | 4 | 5 | 6 |
| 7 | 8 | 9 | 10 | 11 | 12 | 13 |
| 14 | 15 | 16 | 17 | 18 | 19 | 20 |
| 21 | 22 | 23 | 24 | 25 | 26 | 27 |
| 28 | 29 | 30 |   |   |   |   |

# 2026

# The Enemy Does Not Like *Growth*

## July

| S | M | T | W | T | F | S |
|---|---|---|---|---|---|---|
|   |   |   | 1 | 2 | 3 | 4 |
| 5 | 6 | 7 | 8 | 9 | 10 | 11 |
| 12 | 13 | 14 | 15 | 16 | 17 | 18 |
| 19 | 20 | 21 | 22 | 23 | 24 | 25 |
| 26 | 27 | 28 | 29 | 30 | 31 |   |

## August

| S | M | T | W | T | F | S |
|---|---|---|---|---|---|---|
|   |   |   |   |   |   | 1 |
| 2 | 3 | 4 | 5 | 6 | 7 | 8 |
| 9 | 10 | 11 | 12 | 13 | 14 | 15 |
| 16 | 17 | 18 | 19 | 20 | 21 | 22 |
| 23 | 24 | 25 | 26 | 27 | 28 | 29 |
| 30 | 31 |   |   |   |   |   |

## September

| S | M | T | W | T | F | S |
|---|---|---|---|---|---|---|
|   |   | 1 | 2 | 3 | 4 | 5 |
| 6 | 7 | 8 | 9 | 10 | 11 | 12 |
| 13 | 14 | 15 | 16 | 17 | 18 | 19 |
| 20 | 21 | 22 | 23 | 24 | 25 | 26 |
| 27 | 28 | 29 | 30 |   |   |   |

# Jesus gives the best *Gardening* Advice

## October

| S | M | T | W | T | F | S |
|---|---|---|---|---|---|---|
|   |   |   |   | 1 | 2 | 3 |
| 4 | 5 | 6 | 7 | 8 | 9 | 10 |
| 11 | 12 | 13 | 14 | 15 | 16 | 17 |
| 18 | 19 | 20 | 21 | 22 | 23 | 24 |
| 25 | 26 | 27 | 28 | 29 | 30 | 31 |

## November

| S | M | T | W | T | F | S |
|---|---|---|---|---|---|---|
| 1 | 2 | 3 | 4 | 5 | 6 | 7 |
| 8 | 9 | 10 | 11 | 12 | 13 | 14 |
| 15 | 16 | 17 | 18 | 19 | 20 | 21 |
| 22 | 23 | 24 | 25 | 26 | 27 | 28 |
| 29 | 30 |   |   |   |   |   |

## December

| S | M | T | W | T | F | S |
|---|---|---|---|---|---|---|
|   |   | 1 | 2 | 3 | 4 | 5 |
| 6 | 7 | 8 | 9 | 10 | 11 | 12 |
| 13 | 14 | 15 | 16 | 17 | 18 | 19 |
| 20 | 21 | 22 | 23 | 24 | 25 | 26 |
| 27 | 28 | 29 | 30 | 31 |   |   |

**2026**

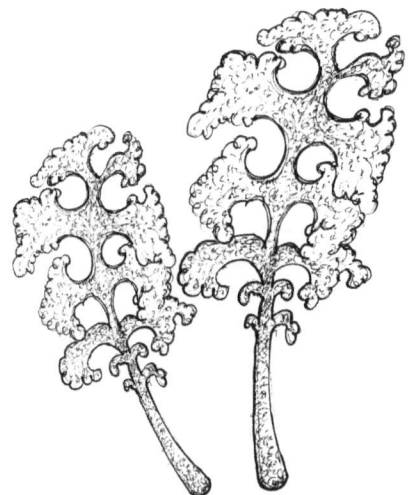

# God's Dream for Me + My Garden

_____

_____

_____

_____

_____

_____

_____

_____

_____

_____

_____

_____

_____

# I am *Planted* Like a Tree

## January

| S | M | T | W | T | F | S |
|---|---|---|---|---|---|---|
|   |   |   |   |   | 1 | 2 |
| 3 | 4 | 5 | 6 | 7 | 8 | 9 |
| 10 | 11 | 12 | 13 | 14 | 15 | 16 |
| 17 | 18 | 19 | 20 | 21 | 22 | 23 |
| 24 | 25 | 26 | 27 | 28 | 29 | 30 |
| 31 |   |   |   |   |   |   |

## February

| S | M | T | W | T | F | S |
|---|---|---|---|---|---|---|
|   | 1 | 2 | 3 | 4 | 5 | 6 |
| 7 | 8 | 9 | 10 | 11 | 12 | 13 |
| 14 | 15 | 16 | 17 | 18 | 19 | 20 |
| 21 | 22 | 23 | 24 | 25 | 26 | 27 |
| 28 |   |   |   |   |   |   |

## March

| S | M | T | W | T | F | S |
|---|---|---|---|---|---|---|
|   | 1 | 2 | 3 | 4 | 5 | 6 |
| 7 | 8 | 9 | 10 | 11 | 12 | 13 |
| 14 | 15 | 16 | 17 | 18 | 19 | 20 |
| 21 | 22 | 23 | 24 | 25 | 26 | 27 |
| 28 | 29 | 30 | 31 |   |   |   |

# Gardening is an activity of the *Future*

## April

| S | M | T | W | T | F | S |
|---|---|---|---|---|---|---|
|   |   |   |   | 1 | 2 | 3 |
| 4 | 5 | 6 | 7 | 8 | 9 | 10 |
| 11 | 12 | 13 | 14 | 15 | 16 | 17 |
| 18 | 19 | 20 | 21 | 22 | 23 | 24 |
| 25 | 26 | 27 | 28 | 29 | 30 |   |

## May

| S | M | T | W | T | F | S |
|---|---|---|---|---|---|---|
|   |   |   |   |   |   | 1 |
| 2 | 3 | 4 | 5 | 6 | 7 | 8 |
| 9 | 10 | 11 | 12 | 13 | 14 | 15 |
| 16 | 17 | 18 | 19 | 20 | 21 | 22 |
| 23 | 24 | 25 | 26 | 27 | 28 | 29 |
| 30 | 31 |   |   |   |   |   |

## June

| S | M | T | W | T | F | S |
|---|---|---|---|---|---|---|
|   |   | 1 | 2 | 3 | 4 | 5 |
| 6 | 7 | 8 | 9 | 10 | 11 | 12 |
| 13 | 14 | 15 | 16 | 17 | 18 | 19 |
| 20 | 21 | 22 | 23 | 24 | 25 | 26 |
| 27 | 28 | 29 | 30 |   |   |   |

# 2027

# As I *Grow* My Garden, I Grow Myself

## July

| S | M | T | W | T | F | S |
|---|---|---|---|---|---|---|
|   |   |   |   | 1 | 2 | 3 |
| 4 | 5 | 6 | 7 | 8 | 9 | 10 |
| 11 | 12 | 13 | 14 | 15 | 16 | 17 |
| 18 | 19 | 20 | 21 | 22 | 23 | 24 |
| 25 | 26 | 27 | 28 | 29 | 30 | 31 |

## August

| S | M | T | W | T | F | S |
|---|---|---|---|---|---|---|
| 1 | 2 | 3 | 4 | 5 | 6 | 7 |
| 8 | 9 | 10 | 11 | 12 | 13 | 14 |
| 15 | 16 | 17 | 18 | 19 | 20 | 21 |
| 22 | 23 | 24 | 25 | 26 | 27 | 28 |
| 29 | 30 | 31 |   |   |   |   |

## September

| S | M | T | W | T | F | S |
|---|---|---|---|---|---|---|
|   |   |   | 1 | 2 | 3 | 4 |
| 5 | 6 | 7 | 8 | 9 | 10 | 11 |
| 12 | 13 | 14 | 15 | 16 | 17 | 18 |
| 19 | 20 | 21 | 22 | 23 | 24 | 25 |
| 26 | 27 | 28 | 29 | 30 |   |   |

# God's Mercy is as tender as a *Flower*

## October

| S | M | T | W | T | F | S |
|---|---|---|---|---|---|---|
|   |   |   |   |   | 1 | 2 |
| 3 | 4 | 5 | 6 | 7 | 8 | 9 |
| 10 | 11 | 12 | 13 | 14 | 15 | 16 |
| 17 | 18 | 19 | 20 | 21 | 22 | 23 |
| 24 | 25 | 26 | 27 | 28 | 29 | 30 |
| 31 |   |   |   |   |   |   |

## November

| S | M | T | W | T | F | S |
|---|---|---|---|---|---|---|
|   | 1 | 2 | 3 | 4 | 5 | 6 |
| 7 | 8 | 9 | 10 | 11 | 12 | 13 |
| 14 | 15 | 16 | 17 | 18 | 19 | 20 |
| 21 | 22 | 23 | 24 | 25 | 26 | 27 |
| 28 | 29 | 30 |   |   |   |   |

## December

| S | M | T | W | T | F | S |
|---|---|---|---|---|---|---|
|   |   |   | 1 | 2 | 3 | 4 |
| 5 | 6 | 7 | 8 | 9 | 10 | 11 |
| 12 | 13 | 14 | 15 | 16 | 17 | 18 |
| 19 | 20 | 21 | 22 | 23 | 24 | 25 |
| 26 | 27 | 28 | 29 | 30 | 31 |   |

# 2027

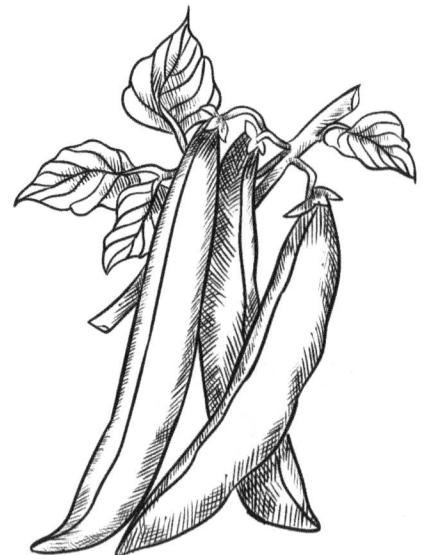

# God's Dream for Me + My Garden

_____

_____

_____

_____

_____

_____

_____

_____

_____

_____

_____

_____

_____

# For Every *Season* There is Help

## January

| S | M | T | W | T | F | S |
|---|---|---|---|---|---|---|
|   |   |   |   |   |   | 1 |
| 2 | 3 | 4 | 5 | 6 | 7 | 8 |
| 9 | 10 | 11 | 12 | 13 | 14 | 15 |
| 16 | 17 | 18 | 19 | 20 | 21 | 22 |
| 23 | 24 | 25 | 26 | 27 | 28 | 29 |
| 30 | 31 |   |   |   |   |   |

## February

| S | M | T | W | T | F | S |
|---|---|---|---|---|---|---|
|   |   | 1 | 2 | 3 | 4 | 5 |
| 6 | 7 | 8 | 9 | 10 | 11 | 12 |
| 13 | 14 | 15 | 16 | 17 | 18 | 19 |
| 20 | 21 | 22 | 23 | 24 | 25 | 26 |
| 27 | 28 | 29 |   |   |   |   |

## March

| S | M | T | W | T | F | S |
|---|---|---|---|---|---|---|
|   |   |   | 1 | 2 | 3 | 4 |
| 5 | 6 | 7 | 8 | 9 | 10 | 11 |
| 12 | 13 | 14 | 15 | 16 | 17 | 18 |
| 19 | 20 | 21 | 22 | 23 | 24 | 25 |
| 26 | 27 | 28 | 29 | 30 | 31 |   |

# My Seasons and Times are in *God's* Hands

## April

| S | M | T | W | T | F | S |
|---|---|---|---|---|---|---|
|   |   |   |   |   |   | 1 |
| 2 | 3 | 4 | 5 | 6 | 7 | 8 |
| 9 | 10 | 11 | 12 | 13 | 14 | 15 |
| 16 | 17 | 18 | 19 | 20 | 21 | 22 |
| 23 | 24 | 25 | 26 | 27 | 28 | 29 |
| 30 |   |   |   |   |   |   |

## May

| S | M | T | W | T | F | S |
|---|---|---|---|---|---|---|
|   | 1 | 2 | 3 | 4 | 5 | 6 |
| 7 | 8 | 9 | 10 | 11 | 12 | 13 |
| 14 | 15 | 16 | 17 | 18 | 19 | 20 |
| 21 | 22 | 23 | 24 | 25 | 26 | 27 |
| 28 | 29 | 30 | 31 |   |   |   |

## June

| S | M | T | W | T | F | S |
|---|---|---|---|---|---|---|
|   |   |   |   | 1 | 2 | 3 |
| 4 | 5 | 6 | 7 | 8 | 9 | 10 |
| 11 | 12 | 13 | 14 | 15 | 16 | 17 |
| 18 | 19 | 20 | 21 | 22 | 23 | 24 |
| 25 | 26 | 27 | 28 | 29 | 30 |   |

# 2028

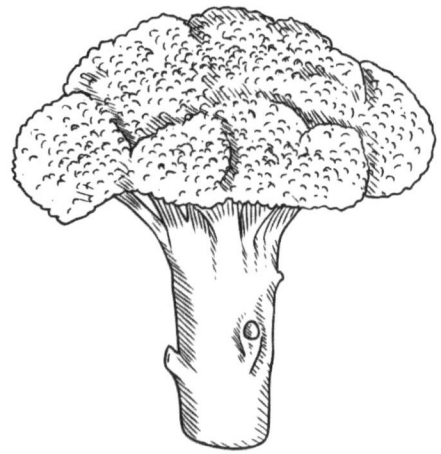

# God will Grow My *Goals*

## July

| S | M | T | W | T | F | S |
|---|---|---|---|---|---|---|
|   |   |   |   |   |   | 1 |
| 2 | 3 | 4 | 5 | 6 | 7 | 8 |
| 9 | 10 | 11 | 12 | 13 | 14 | 15 |
| 16 | 17 | 18 | 19 | 20 | 21 | 22 |
| 23 | 24 | 25 | 26 | 27 | 28 | 29 |
| 30 | 31 |   |   |   |   |   |

## August

| S | M | T | W | T | F | S |
|---|---|---|---|---|---|---|
|   |   | 1 | 2 | 3 | 4 | 5 |
| 6 | 7 | 8 | 9 | 10 | 11 | 12 |
| 13 | 14 | 15 | 16 | 17 | 18 | 19 |
| 20 | 21 | 22 | 23 | 24 | 25 | 26 |
| 27 | 28 | 29 | 30 | 31 |   |   |

## September

| S | M | T | W | T | F | S |
|---|---|---|---|---|---|---|
|   |   |   |   |   | 1 | 2 |
| 3 | 4 | 5 | 6 | 7 | 8 | 9 |
| 10 | 11 | 12 | 13 | 14 | 15 | 16 |
| 17 | 18 | 19 | 20 | 21 | 22 | 23 |
| 24 | 25 | 26 | 27 | 28 | 29 | 30 |

# God Sees my Present, Past, and *Future*

## October

| S | M | T | W | T | F | S |
|---|---|---|---|---|---|---|
| 1 | 2 | 3 | 4 | 5 | 6 | 7 |
| 8 | 9 | 10 | 11 | 12 | 13 | 14 |
| 15 | 16 | 17 | 18 | 19 | 20 | 21 |
| 22 | 23 | 24 | 25 | 26 | 27 | 28 |
| 29 | 30 | 31 |   |   |   |   |

## November

| S | M | T | W | T | F | S |
|---|---|---|---|---|---|---|
|   |   |   | 1 | 2 | 3 | 4 |
| 5 | 6 | 7 | 8 | 9 | 10 | 11 |
| 12 | 13 | 14 | 15 | 16 | 17 | 18 |
| 19 | 20 | 21 | 22 | 23 | 24 | 25 |
| 26 | 27 | 28 | 29 | 30 |   |   |

## December

| S | M | T | W | T | F | S |
|---|---|---|---|---|---|---|
|   |   |   |   |   | 1 | 2 |
| 3 | 4 | 5 | 6 | 7 | 8 | 9 |
| 10 | 11 | 12 | 13 | 14 | 15 | 16 |
| 17 | 18 | 19 | 20 | 21 | 22 | 23 |
| 24 | 25 | 26 | 27 | 28 | 29 | 30 |
| 31 |   |   |   |   |   |   |

# 2028

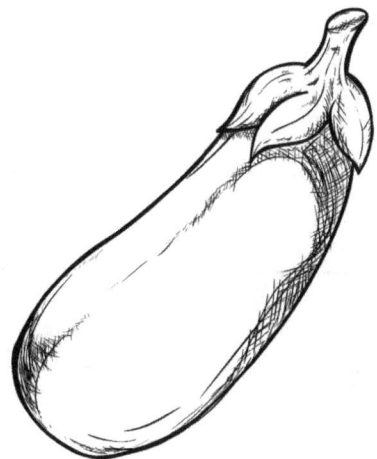

# God's Dream For Me + My Garden

# My Baskets will *Overflow*

## January

| S | M | T | W | T | F | S |
|---|---|---|---|---|---|---|
|  | 1 | 2 | 3 | 4 | 5 | 6 |
| 7 | 8 | 9 | 10 | 11 | 12 | 13 |
| 14 | 15 | 16 | 17 | 18 | 19 | 20 |
| 21 | 22 | 23 | 24 | 25 | 26 | 27 |
| 28 | 29 | 30 | 31 |  |  |  |

## February

| S | M | T | W | T | F | S |
|---|---|---|---|---|---|---|
|  |  |  |  | 1 | 2 | 3 |
| 4 | 5 | 6 | 7 | 8 | 9 | 10 |
| 11 | 12 | 13 | 14 | 15 | 16 | 17 |
| 18 | 19 | 20 | 21 | 22 | 23 | 24 |
| 25 | 26 | 27 | 28 |  |  |  |

## March

| S | M | T | W | T | F | S |
|---|---|---|---|---|---|---|
|  |  |  |  | 1 | 2 | 3 |
| 4 | 5 | 6 | 7 | 8 | 9 | 10 |
| 11 | 12 | 13 | 14 | 15 | 16 | 17 |
| 18 | 19 | 20 | 21 | 22 | 23 | 24 |
| 25 | 26 | 27 | 28 | 29 | 30 | 31 |

# The Threshing Floor is *Perfecting* Me

## April

| S | M | T | W | T | F | S |
|---|---|---|---|---|---|---|
| 1 | 2 | 3 | 4 | 5 | 6 | 7 |
| 8 | 9 | 10 | 11 | 12 | 13 | 14 |
| 15 | 16 | 17 | 18 | 19 | 20 | 21 |
| 22 | 23 | 24 | 25 | 26 | 27 | 28 |
| 29 | 30 |  |  |  |  |  |

## May

| S | M | T | W | T | F | S |
|---|---|---|---|---|---|---|
|  |  | 1 | 2 | 3 | 4 | 5 |
| 6 | 7 | 8 | 9 | 10 | 11 | 12 |
| 13 | 14 | 15 | 16 | 17 | 18 | 19 |
| 20 | 21 | 22 | 23 | 24 | 25 | 26 |
| 27 | 28 | 29 | 30 | 31 |  |  |

## June

| S | M | T | W | T | F | S |
|---|---|---|---|---|---|---|
|  |  |  |  |  | 1 | 2 |
| 3 | 4 | 5 | 6 | 7 | 8 | 9 |
| 10 | 11 | 12 | 13 | 14 | 15 | 16 |
| 17 | 18 | 19 | 20 | 21 | 22 | 23 |
| 24 | 25 | 26 | 27 | 28 | 29 | 30 |

# 2029

# I will be as a watered *Garden*

## July
| S | M | T | W | T | F | S |
|---|---|---|---|---|---|---|
| 1 | 2 | 3 | 4 | 5 | 6 | 7 |
| 8 | 9 | 10 | 11 | 12 | 13 | 14 |
| 15 | 16 | 17 | 18 | 19 | 20 | 21 |
| 22 | 23 | 24 | 25 | 26 | 27 | 28 |
| 29 | 30 | 31 | | | | |

## August
| S | M | T | W | T | F | S |
|---|---|---|---|---|---|---|
| | | | 1 | 2 | 3 | 4 |
| 5 | 6 | 7 | 8 | 9 | 10 | 11 |
| 12 | 13 | 14 | 15 | 16 | 17 | 18 |
| 19 | 20 | 21 | 22 | 23 | 24 | 25 |
| 26 | 27 | 28 | 29 | 30 | 31 | |

## September
| S | M | T | W | T | F | S |
|---|---|---|---|---|---|---|
| | | | | | | 1 |
| 2 | 3 | 4 | 5 | 6 | 7 | 8 |
| 9 | 10 | 11 | 12 | 13 | 14 | 15 |
| 16 | 17 | 18 | 19 | 20 | 21 | 22 |
| 23 | 24 | 25 | 26 | 27 | 28 | 29 |
| 30 | | | | | | |

# I tend to my prayers as I tend to my *Garden*

## October
| S | M | T | W | T | F | S |
|---|---|---|---|---|---|---|
| | 1 | 2 | 3 | 4 | 5 | 6 |
| 7 | 8 | 9 | 10 | 11 | 12 | 13 |
| 14 | 15 | 16 | 17 | 18 | 19 | 20 |
| 21 | 22 | 23 | 24 | 25 | 26 | 27 |
| 28 | 29 | 30 | 31 | | | |

## November
| S | M | T | W | T | F | S |
|---|---|---|---|---|---|---|
| | | | | 1 | 2 | 3 |
| 4 | 5 | 6 | 7 | 8 | 9 | 10 |
| 11 | 12 | 13 | 14 | 15 | 16 | 17 |
| 18 | 19 | 20 | 21 | 22 | 23 | 24 |
| 25 | 26 | 27 | 28 | 29 | 30 | |

## December
| S | M | T | W | T | F | S |
|---|---|---|---|---|---|---|
| | | | | | | 1 |
| 2 | 3 | 4 | 5 | 6 | 7 | 8 |
| 9 | 10 | 11 | 12 | 13 | 14 | 15 |
| 16 | 17 | 18 | 19 | 20 | 21 | 22 |
| 23 | 24 | 25 | 26 | 27 | 28 | 29 |
| 30 | 31 | | | | | |

# 2029

# God's Dream For Me + My Garden

# My Garden will be *Blessed* in Season

## January

| S | M | T | W | T | F | S |
|---|---|---|---|---|---|---|
|   |   | 1 | 2 | 3 | 4 | 5 |
| 6 | 7 | 8 | 9 | 10 | 11 | 12 |
| 13 | 14 | 15 | 16 | 17 | 18 | 19 |
| 20 | 21 | 22 | 23 | 24 | 25 | 26 |
| 27 | 28 | 29 | 30 | 31 |   |   |

## February

| S | M | T | W | T | F | S |
|---|---|---|---|---|---|---|
|   |   |   |   |   | 1 | 2 |
| 3 | 4 | 5 | 6 | 7 | 8 | 9 |
| 10 | 11 | 12 | 13 | 14 | 15 | 16 |
| 17 | 18 | 19 | 20 | 21 | 22 | 23 |
| 24 | 25 | 26 | 27 | 28 |   |   |

## March

| S | M | T | W | T | F | S |
|---|---|---|---|---|---|---|
|   |   |   |   |   | 1 | 2 |
| 3 | 4 | 5 | 6 | 7 | 8 | 9 |
| 10 | 11 | 12 | 13 | 14 | 15 | 16 |
| 17 | 18 | 19 | 20 | 21 | 22 | 23 |
| 24 | 25 | 26 | 27 | 28 | 29 | 30 |
| 31 |   |   |   |   |   |   |

# I am Blessed in the Fields of *Golden* Grain

## April

| S | M | T | W | T | F | S |
|---|---|---|---|---|---|---|
|   | 1 | 2 | 3 | 4 | 5 | 6 |
| 7 | 8 | 9 | 10 | 11 | 12 | 13 |
| 14 | 15 | 16 | 17 | 18 | 19 | 20 |
| 21 | 22 | 23 | 24 | 25 | 26 | 27 |
| 28 | 29 | 30 |   |   |   |   |

## May

| S | M | T | W | T | F | S |
|---|---|---|---|---|---|---|
|   |   |   | 1 | 2 | 3 | 4 |
| 5 | 6 | 7 | 8 | 9 | 10 | 11 |
| 12 | 13 | 14 | 15 | 16 | 17 | 18 |
| 19 | 20 | 21 | 22 | 23 | 24 | 25 |
| 26 | 27 | 28 | 29 | 30 | 31 |   |

## June

| S | M | T | W | T | F | S |
|---|---|---|---|---|---|---|
|   |   |   |   |   |   | 1 |
| 2 | 3 | 4 | 5 | 6 | 7 | 8 |
| 9 | 10 | 11 | 12 | 13 | 14 | 15 |
| 16 | 17 | 18 | 19 | 20 | 21 | 22 |
| 23 | 24 | 25 | 26 | 27 | 28 | 29 |
| 30 |   |   |   |   |   |   |

# 2030

# My Garden Grows *Abundance* From Heaven

## July

| S | M | T | W | T | F | S |
|---|---|---|---|---|---|---|
|   | 1 | 2 | 3 | 4 | 5 | 6 |
| 7 | 8 | 9 | 10 | 11 | 12 | 13 |
| 14 | 15 | 16 | 17 | 18 | 19 | 20 |
| 21 | 22 | 23 | 24 | 25 | 26 | 27 |
| 28 | 29 | 30 | 31 |   |   |   |

## August

| S | M | T | W | T | F | S |
|---|---|---|---|---|---|---|
|   |   |   |   | 1 | 2 | 3 |
| 4 | 5 | 6 | 7 | 8 | 9 | 10 |
| 11 | 12 | 13 | 14 | 15 | 16 | 17 |
| 18 | 19 | 20 | 21 | 22 | 23 | 24 |
| 25 | 26 | 27 | 28 | 29 | 30 | 31 |

## September

| S | M | T | W | T | F | S |
|---|---|---|---|---|---|---|
| 1 | 2 | 3 | 4 | 5 | 6 | 7 |
| 8 | 9 | 10 | 11 | 12 | 13 | 14 |
| 15 | 16 | 17 | 18 | 19 | 20 | 21 |
| 22 | 23 | 24 | 25 | 26 | 27 | 28 |
| 29 | 30 |   |   |   |   |   |

# I am Blessed Going in and *Out* of my Garden

## October

| S | M | T | W | T | F | S |
|---|---|---|---|---|---|---|
|   | 1 | 2 | 3 | 4 | 5 |   |
| 6 | 7 | 8 | 9 | 10 | 11 | 12 |
| 13 | 14 | 15 | 16 | 17 | 18 | 19 |
| 20 | 21 | 22 | 23 | 24 | 25 | 26 |
| 27 | 28 | 29 | 30 | 31 |   |   |

## November

| S | M | T | W | T | F | S |
|---|---|---|---|---|---|---|
|   |   |   |   |   | 1 | 2 |
| 3 | 4 | 5 | 6 | 7 | 8 | 9 |
| 10 | 11 | 12 | 13 | 14 | 15 | 16 |
| 17 | 18 | 19 | 20 | 21 | 22 | 23 |
| 24 | 25 | 26 | 27 | 28 | 29 | 30 |

## December

| S | M | T | W | T | F | S |
|---|---|---|---|---|---|---|
| 1 | 2 | 3 | 4 | 5 | 6 | 7 |
| 8 | 9 | 10 | 11 | 12 | 13 | 14 |
| 15 | 16 | 17 | 18 | 19 | 20 | 21 |
| 22 | 23 | 24 | 25 | 26 | 27 | 28 |
| 29 | 30 | 31 |   |   |   |   |

# 2030

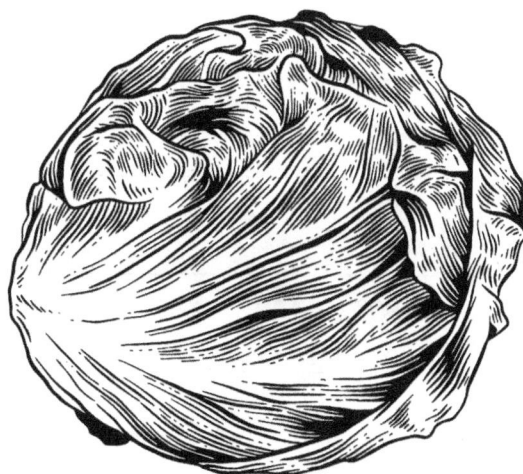

# Gods Dream For Me + My Garden

_____

_____

_____

_____

_____

_____

_____

_____

_____

_____

_____

_____

_____

_____

# Thank You!

As I contemplate the profound concept of God growing gardens and our existence as His beloved creations, my heart swells with awe and gratitude.

The metaphor of a divine gardener tending to the growth of our souls fills me with hope and reassurance, reminding me that we are not alone in this journey of life. Just as a skilled gardener nurtures each plant with care and attention, so too does God, in His infinite wisdom and love, guide us, prune us, and help us blossom into the unique individuals we were meant to be.

May we always strive to embrace God's gentle touch, trusting that through His divine cultivation, we can flourish, spreading beauty, love, and goodness to a world yearning for it.

As we grow alongside the divine Gardener, may our lives become living testaments to His grace, vibrant gardens that inspire others to seek their own connection with the God the Gardener.

God. Growth. Gardens. Goals.